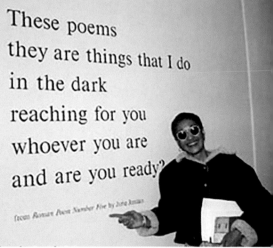

These poems
they are things that I do
in the dark
reaching for you
whoever you are
and are you ready?

(from Roman Poem Number Five by June Jordan)

If you will bear with me
for a few minutes I
will share with you
a few
of the 30,117 uses to which
the lowly peanut has been
put
by me
since yesterday afternoon.

Looking down to my feet you will notice
sensible shoelaces of unadulterated
peanut leaf composition that is biodegradable
in the extreme
as well as pliable
enough for on and off again regular
habits of shoe using throughout one
to two weeks.

To your left you may observe the amazing
masterpiece reproduction cleverly priced
of several million peanut shell chips
that accurately represent the colors of the aug
Overhead you may notice a squadron
of peanut B-52 bombers flying due
at an altitude of 20,004 feet give
a few leguminous variables,

I would extend my hand in greeting to you
except for the fact that I am holding a red
supply of dry Roasted and unsalted peanuts
guaranteed to accelerate protein assimi
at a calculable Rate
by my pocket peanut calculat

CIVIL WARS

"A major and indispensable reading experience." —ALICE WALKER

OBSERVATIONS FROM THE FRONT LINES OF AMERICA

with a new introduction by the author

JUNE JORDAN

→3 　　　→3A 　　　→4 　　　→4A 　　　→5

A 　　　→9 　　　→9A 　　　→10 　　　→10A 　　　→11

→15 　　　→15A 　　　→16 　　　→16A 　　　→17

THE ESSENTIAL JUNE JORDAN

BOOKS BY JUNE JORDAN

Who Look at Me (1969)

Soulscript: A Collection of African American Poetry, editor (1970, 2004)

The Voice of the Children, collected by June Jordan and Terri Bush (1970)

His Own Where (1971)

Some Changes (1971)

Fannie Lou Hamer (1972)

Dry Victories (1972)

New Days: Poems of Exile and Return (1974)

New Life: New Room (1975)

Things that I Do in the Dark: Selected Poems (1977)

Passion: New Poems 1977–1980 (1980)

Kimako's Story (1981)

Civil Wars: Observations from the Front Lines of America (1981, 1996)

Living Room: New Poems (1985)

On Call: Political Essays (1985)

Lyrical Campaigns: Selected Poems (1989)

Moving Towards Home: Political Essays (1989)

Naming Our Destiny: New and Selected Poems (1989)

Technical Difficulties: African-American Notes on the State of the Union (1992)

Haruko/Love Poems (1994)

I Was Looking at the Ceiling and Then I Saw the Sky (1995)

June Jordan's Poetry for the People: A Revolutionary Blueprint (1995)

Kissing God Goodbye: Poems 1991–1997 (1997)

Affirmative Acts: Political Essays (1998)

Soldier: A Poet's Childhood (2000)

Some of Us Did Not Die: New and Selected Essays (2002)

Directed by Desire: The Collected Poems of June Jordan, edited by
Jan Heller Levi and Sara Miles (2005)

Life as Activism: June Jordan's Writings from "The Progressive,"
edited by Stacy Russo (2014)

We're On: A June Jordan Reader, edited by Christoph Keller and
Jan Heller Levi (2017)

Life Studies: 1966–1976, edited by Conor Tomás Reed and
Talia Shalev (2017)

Only Our Hearts Will Argue Hard: Selected Poems, edited by
Christoph Keller (2019)

The Essential June Jordan, edited by Jan Heller Levi and
Christoph Keller (2021)

THE ESSENTIAL
JUNE JORDAN

EDITED BY JAN HELLER LEVI AND CHRISTOPH KELLER
AFTERWORD BY JERICHO BROWN

COPPER CANYON PRESS
PORT TOWNSEND, WASHINGTON

Cover art: June Jordan, circa 1968. Photo by Louise Bernikow. June Jordan Papers, Schlesinger Library, Radcliffe Institute.

Copper Canyon Press is in residence at Fort Worden State Park in Port Townsend, Washington, under the auspices of Centrum. Centrum is a gathering place for artists and creative thinkers from around the world, students of all ages and backgrounds, and audiences seeking extraordinary cultural enrichment.

Library of Congress Cataloging-in-Publication Data
Names: Jordan, June, 1936–2002, author. | Levi, Jan Heller, editor. |
    Keller, Christoph, 1963– editor. | Brown, Jericho, writer of afterword.
Title: The essential June Jordan / edited by Jan Heller Levi and Christoph
    Keller ; afterword by Jericho Brown.
Description: Port Townsend, Washington : Copper Canyon Press, [2021] |
    Summary: "A collection drawn from June Jordan's previous books"—
    Provided by publisher.
Identifiers: LCCN 2020053902 | ISBN 9781556596209 (paperback)
Subjects: LCGFT: Poetry.
Classification: LCC PS3560.O73 E87 2021 | DDC 811/.54—dc23
LC record available at https://lccn.loc.gov/2020053902

98765432

Copper Canyon Press
Post Office Box 271
Port Townsend, Washington 98368
www.coppercanyonpress.org

This book is dedicated to Christopher Meyer, and to the next generation—and the next, and the next—of readers and writers inspired by June Jordan.

And so poetry is not a shopping list, a casual disquisition on the colors of the sky, a soporific daydream, or bumpersticker sloganeering. Poetry is a political action undertaken for the sake of information, the faith, the exorcism, and the lyrical invention, that telling the truth makes possible. Poetry means taking control of the language of your life. Good poems can interdict a suicide, rescue a love affair, and build a revolution in which speaking and listening to somebody becomes the first and last purpose to every social encounter.

JUNE JORDAN

CONTENTS

ľ·ĵ

ľ·ĵ

ι·ĵ

ι·ĵ

ƚ∙ĵ

What a privilege it is to select the "essential" June Jordan, and what a challenge—what of her work *isn't* essential? Reading June again for 2021 publication, we were struck by how many times we said to each other, "This could have been written *now!*" That's the art and urgency of this extraordinary poet, activist, thinker, lover, fighter, and teacher who took up the daunting task of telling us who she was and, more importantly, who *we* are.

Jordan's words go where they're called for, where they're needed. Wherever the way things are is different from the way things should be, you'll find June Jordan. Sometimes her words arrive in the form of a strict and swooning Elizabethan sonnet or as a translation of Shakespeare's sonnet 116 into the insurrectionary splendor and clarity of Black English. Sometimes her words are a praise poem, sometimes an indictment. Sometimes they're a wake-up call, sometimes a lullaby. Whatever she writes, it's immediate, truthful, and *real.*

Love and passion are important words in this political poet's artistry. Her love poems are voluptuous declarations of touch and feel and be and know, heat and heartbreak—simultaneously languid, tender, taut, deliberate, delicate, spontaneous, crafted—and crafty!—and, in the tradition of the best love poems, persuasive. She was, it is astonishing to realize, the first African American woman to publish a book of love poems, her *Haruko/Love Poems* (1994). And in that book, she reprints her stunning "I Must Become a Menace to My Enemies" from *Things that I Do in the Dark* (1977), reconfirming that a poem can be both a passionate declaration of love and a fierce political call to arms. (Next year, we're delighted to say, Copper Canyon will reissue June's classic *Passion,* from 1980, with its famous introductory essay "For the Sake of People's Poetry: Walt Whitman and the Rest of Us.")

The traditional Selected Poems presents the poet's work book by book, in chronological order. But we wanted to do something else: to give you the June Jordan of then and the June Jordan of now, together. Jordan herself inspired our experiment. In *Things that I Do in the Dark,* she brought old and new poems together in newly named sections. For *Naming Our Destiny* (1989) she selected directly from *Things that I Do in the Dark* and *not* from her first three volumes of poetry, emphasizing, twelve years later, how important that experiment was. As we began our reorchestrating— or maybe our remixing—of her work, we also took courage knowing her collected poems, *Directed by Desire* (2005), is still in print with Copper Canyon. So if you don't find your favorite June Jordan poem here, or you want to return to reading her year by year, you can pick up a copy of *Directed by Desire.*

We've added to this book a two-part ideogram—"j. j."—which you'll find on the pages between the sections. June Jordan signed all her letters, cards, and poems to friends this way. We thought it fitting that her readers get to know her ideogram, which stands for what we called her and she called herself to us: "jay jay." Our invented character names her and what she believed in and taught us to work for: joy and justice.

The Essential June Jordan begins with an epigraph poem, an excerpt from her remarkable first book, *Who Look at Me* (1969)—a single, long ekphrastic poem that was companioned with repro- ductions of twenty-seven paintings of African Americans, many of them the work of African American artists such as Charles Alston, John Wilson, and Hughie Lee-Smith. *Who Look at Me,* in its entirety with its images, is without a doubt an American treasure, an equal of Jacob Lawrence's 1940–41 *The Migration Series. Who Look at Me* also anticipates the powerful, provocative reframing of Black/White history by outstanding African American visual artists including Kara Walker, Kerry James Marshall, Mickalene Thomas, Xaviera Simmons, Vanessa German, David Hammons, Carrie Mae Weems, and Betye Saar.

The next section and the sixth are then organized chronologically, but with a twist. For these we selected just one poem from each subsequent book, from *Some Changes* (1971) to *Last Poems* (composed 1997–2001 and published in *Directed by Desire*), to illuminate the grand sweep of her life's work. In the middle sections, we experimented with association, putting early poems together with later ones, and we were excited to see how June spoke to June—and to her readers—across the years. For example, when her "On the Black Family" from *New Days* (1974), "Racial Profile #3" from *Last Poems,* and "1978" from *Passion* arrive one after another, each becomes freshly immediate. The sparks fly when "Song of the Law Abiding Citizen" sits beside "Letter to the Local Police," and they both throw down the gauntlet in her brilliant rap, "Owed to Eminem." Then "Owed to Eminem" strikes a match that blazes in "A Song of Sojourner Truth." And there's the unflinching description of massacred Native Americans and a ravaged landscape in "Poem for Nana," which echoes the piercingly specific description of her mastectomy-ravaged breast in "To Be Continued:." Can you see how Jordan's eye is positively surgical? Our section dividers are six of Jordan's tour-de-force long poems (several of which ended her books), and these selections are in chronological order too.

We call the book's last section "Poems Against a Conclusion." Again we took our cue from the poet, who ended *New Days* (1974) with a section called "Poem Against a Conclusion." The section consisted of the single poem "These Poems," which she reprinted in several books as a kind of signature; Jan and Sara Miles did the same to open *Directed by Desire.* It seemed fitting to include this signature here, alongside other poems reminding us that June Jordan, who died of breast cancer in 2002, is absolutely not gone.

We're also excited to include, in section six, four previously unpublished poems that we discovered in the process of putting together this book. These are vintage Jordan texts written toward the end of June's life some twenty-five years ago. But they sound like today: "I'm serious about I don't wanna die / from /

mainstream contamination," she writes in "Manifesto of the Rubber Gloves." Are they essential? Well, let's check in on that in another decade or two.

~

We thank, above all, June Jordan, for a lifetime of writing essential poems. We also thank Sara Miles, coexecutor of the June M. Jordan Literary Estate, whose insight, intelligence, and steadfast good sense helped make this book possible and who continues to keep June's work and spirit alive in the world. We are grateful to June's friends and students who told us what their essential poems are and helped make this an even richer collection than we might have created without them. Our gratitude also to Jericho Brown for his insightful and moving afterword. Finally, we thank the folks at Copper Canyon—Michael Wiegers, John Pierce, designer Phil Kovacevich, copy editor Jessica Roeder, publicist Laura Buccieri, and copublisher George Knotek—and many others behind the scenes, who put their enormous care, devotion, enthusiasm, and excellence into creating *The Essential June Jordan.*

JAN HELLER LEVI & CHRISTOPH KELLER,
OCTOBER 2020

THE ESSENTIAL JUNE JORDAN

from Who Look at Me

Who would paint a people
black or white?

~

For my own I have held
where nothing showed me how
where finally I left alone
to trace another destination

~

A white stare splits the air
by blindness on the subway
in department stores
The Elevator
                    (that unswerving ride
where man ignores the brother
by his side)

A white stare splits obliterates
the nerve-wrung wrist from work
the breaking ankle or
the turning glory
of a spine

~

Is that how we look to you
a partial nothing clearly real?

who see a solid clarity
of feature
size and shape of some

one head
an unmistaken nose
the fact of afternoon
as darkening
his candle eyes

Older men with swollen neck

(when they finally sit down
who will stand up
for them?)

I cannot remember nor imagine pretty
people treat me
like a doublejointed stick

                              WHO LOOK AT ME
                              WHO SEE

the tempering sweetness
of a little girl who wears
her first pair of earrings
and a red dress

the grace of a boy removing
a white mask he makes beautiful

Iron grille across the glass
and frames of motion closed or
charred or closed

The axe lies on the ground
She listening to his coming sound

him
just touching his feet
powerful and wary

anonymous and normal
parents and their offspring
posed in formal

~

I am

impossible to explain
remote from old and new interpretations
and yet
not exactly

~

look at the stranger as

he lies more gray than black
on that colorquilt
that
(everyone will say)
seems bright beside him

look
black sailors on the light
green sea the sky keeps blue
the wind blows high
and hard at night
for anyhow anywhere new

~

Who see starvation at the table
lines of men no work to do
my mother ironing a shirt?

Who see a frozen skin the midnight
of the winter and the hallway cold
to kill you like the dirt?

where kids buy soda pop
in shoeshine parlors
barber shops so they can hear
some laughing

Who look at me?

Who see the children
on their street the torn down door the wall
complete an early losing
                              games of ball
the search to find
a fatherhood a mothering of mind
a multimillion multicolored mirror
of an honest humankind?

                    ~

look close
and see me black man mouth
for breathing (North and South)
A MAN

I am black alive and looking back at you.

                    ~

see me brown girl throat
that throbs from servitude

see me hearing fragile
leap
and lead a black boy
reckless to succeed
to wrap my pride
around tomorrow and to go
there
without fearing

see me darkly covered ribs
around my heart across my skull
thin skin protects the part
that dulls from longing

~

Who see the block we face
the thousand miles of solid alabaster space
inscribed keep off keep out don't touch
and Wait Some More for Half as Much?

~

To begin is no more agony
than opening your hand

[•]

If You Saw a Negro Lady

If you saw a Negro lady
sitting on a Tuesday
near the whirl-sludge doors of
Horn & Hardart on the main drag
of downtown Brooklyn

solitary and conspicuous as plain
and neat as walls impossible to
fresco and you watched her self-
conscious features shape about
a Horn & Hardart teaspoon
with a pucker from a cartoon

she would not understand
with spine as straight and solid
as her years of bending over floors
allowed

skin cleared of interest by a ruthless
soap   nails square and yellowclean
from metal files

sitting in a forty-year-old flush
of solitude and prickling
from the new white cotton blouse
concealing nothing she had ever noticed
even when she bathed and never
hummed a bathtub tune nor knew one

If you saw her square
above the dirty
mopped-on antiseptic floors

before the rag-wiped table tops

little finger   broad and stiff
in heavy emulation of a cockney

mannerism
would you turn her treat
into surprise
observing

happy birthday

Roman Poem Number Thirteen

For Eddie

Only our hearts will argue hard
against the small lights letting in the news
and who can choose between the worst possibility
and the last
between the winners of the wars against the breathing
and the last
war everyone will lose
and who can choose between the dry gas
domination of the future
and the past
between the consequences of the killers
and the past
of all the killing? There
is no choice in these.
Your voice
breaks very close to me my love.

I Must Become a Menace to My Enemies

Dedicated to the Poet Agostinho Neto, President
of The People's Republic of Angola: 1976

1

I will no longer lightly walk behind
a one of you who fear me:
             Be afraid.
I plan to give you reasons for your jumpy fits
and facial tics
I will not walk politely on the pavements anymore
and this is dedicated in particular
to those who hear my footsteps
or the insubstantial rattling of my grocery
cart
then turn around
see me
and hurry on
away from this impressive terror I must be:
I plan to blossom bloody on an afternoon
surrounded by my comrades singing
terrible revenge in merciless
accelerating
rhythms
But
I have watched a blind man studying his face.
I have set the table in the evening and sat down
to eat the news.
Regularly
I have gone to sleep.
There is no one to forgive me.
The dead do not give a damn.

14   THINGS THAT I DO IN THE DARK, 1977

I live like a lover
who drops her dime into the phone
just as the subway shakes into the station
wasting her message
canceling the question of her call:

fulminating or forgetful but late
and always after the fact that could save or
condemn me

I must become the action of my fate.

2

How many of my brothers and my sisters
will they kill
before I teach myself
retaliation?
Shall we pick a number?
South Africa for instance:
do we agree that more than ten thousand
in less than a year but that less than
five thousand slaughtered in more than six
months will
WHAT IS THE MATTER WITH ME?

I must become a menace to my enemies.

3

And if I
if I ever let you slide
who should be extirpated from my universe
who should be cauterized from earth
completely

(lawandorder jerkoffs of the first the
terrorist degree)
then let my body fail my soul
in its bedeviled lecheries

And if I
if I ever let love go
because the hatred and the whisperings
become a phantom dictate I o-
bey in lieu of impulse and realities
(the blossoming flamingos of my
wild mimosa trees)
then let love freeze me
out.

I must become
I must become a menace to my enemies.

Poem about My Rights

Even tonight and I need to take a walk and clear
my head about this poem about why I can't
go out without changing my clothes my shoes
my body posture my gender identity my age
my status as a woman alone in the evening/
alone on the streets/alone not being the point/
the point being that I can't do what I want
to do with my own body because I am the wrong
sex the wrong age the wrong skin and
suppose it was not here in the city but down on the beach/
or far into the woods and I wanted to go
there by myself thinking about God/or thinking
about children or thinking about the world/all of it
disclosed by the stars and the silence:
I could not go and I could not think and I could not
stay there
alone
as I need to be
alone because I can't do what I want to do with my own
body and
who in the hell set things up
like this
and in France they say if the guy penetrates
but does not ejaculate then he did not rape me
and if after stabbing him if after screams if
after begging the bastard and if even after smashing
a hammer to his head if even after that if he
and his buddies fuck me after that
then I consented and there was
no rape because finally you understand finally
they fucked me over because I was wrong I was

wrong again to be me being me where I was/wrong
to be who I am
which is exactly like South Africa
penetrating into Namibia penetrating into
Angola and does that mean I mean how do you know if
Pretoria ejaculates what will the evidence look like the
proof of the monster jackboot ejaculation on Blackland
and if
after Namibia and if after Angola and if after Zimbabwe
and if after all of my kinsmen and women resist even to
self-immolation of the villages and if after that
we lose nevertheless what will the big boys say will they
claim my consent:
Do You Follow Me: We are the wrong people of
the wrong skin on the wrong continent and what
in the hell is everybody being reasonable about
and according to the *Times* this week
back in 1966 the C.I.A. decided that they had this problem
and the problem was a man named Nkrumah so they
killed him and before that it was Patrice Lumumba
and before that it was my father on the campus
of my Ivy League school and my father afraid
to walk into the cafeteria because he said he
was wrong the wrong age the wrong skin the wrong
gender identity and he was paying my tuition and
before that
it was my father saying I was wrong saying that
I should have been a boy because he wanted one/a
boy and that I should have been lighter skinned and
that I should have had straighter hair and that
I should not be so boy crazy but instead I should
just be one/a boy and before that
it was my mother pleading plastic surgery for
my nose and braces for my teeth and telling me

to let the books loose to let them loose in other
words
I am very familiar with the problems of the C.I.A.
and the problems of South Africa and the problems
of Exxon Corporation and the problems of white
America in general and the problems of the teachers
and the preachers and the F.B.I. and the social
workers and my particular Mom and Dad/I am very
familiar with the problems because the problems
turn out to be
me
I am the history of rape
I am the history of the rejection of who I am
I am the history of the terrorized incarceration of
my self
I am the history of battery assault and limitless
armies against whatever I want to do with my mind
and my body and my soul and
whether it's about walking out at night
or whether it's about the love that I feel or
whether it's about the sanctity of my vagina or
the sanctity of my national boundaries
or the sanctity of my leaders or the sanctity
of each and every desire
that I know from my personal and idiosyncratic
and indisputably single and singular heart
I have been raped
be-
cause I have been wrong the wrong sex the wrong age
the wrong skin the wrong nose the wrong hair the
wrong need the wrong dream the wrong geographic
the wrong sartorial I
I have been the meaning of rape
I have been the problem everyone seeks to

eliminate by forced
penetration with or without the evidence of slime and/
but let this be unmistakable this poem
is not consent I do not consent
to my mother to my father to the teachers to
the F.B.I. to South Africa to Bedford-Stuy
to Park Avenue to American Airlines to the hardon
idlers on the corners to the sneaky creeps in
cars
I am not wrong: Wrong is not my name
My name is my own my own my own
and I can't tell you who the hell set things up like this
but I can tell you that from now on my resistance
my simple and daily and nightly self-determination
may very well cost you your life

A Runaway Li'l Bit Poem

Sometimes DeLiza get so crazy she omit
the bebop from the concrete she intimidate
the music she excruciate the whiskey she
obliterate the blow she sneeze
hypothetical at sex

Sometimes DeLiza get so crazy she abstruse
about a bar-be-cue ribs wonder-white-bread
sandwich in the car with hot sauce
make the eyes roll right to where you are
fastidious among the fried-up chicken wings

Sometimes DeLiza get so crazy she exasperate
on do they hook it up they being Ingrid
Bergman and some paranoid schizophrenic Mister
Gregory Peck-peck: Do
they hook it up?

Sometimes DeLiza get so crazy she drive
right across the water flying champagne bottles
from the bridge she last drink to close the bars she
holler kissey lips she laugh she let
you walk yourself away:

Sometimes DeLiza get so crazy!

Poem at the Midnight of My Life

I never thought that I would live forever:
Now I light a cigarette
surprised by pleasures lasting past
predictions from the hemorrhaging of fears
and I reflect on faces soft above my own
in love

The implications of all heated ecstasy that I have known
despite the soldier fist on broken bone
despite the small eyes shrinking flesh to stone
surround me in this tender solitude
like teenage choirs of gullibility
and guts

(How many bottles of beer will it take
to make a baby?)

I understand how nothing ever happens on a one-
plus-one equals anything predictable/
how time rolls
drunk around the curvilinear conventions
of a virgin
and eventual as passion's lapse
just peters out
indefinite

(92 bottles of beer on the wall
92 bottles of beer)

                    how sorry brings you
to the graveside
on an afternoon of trees entirely alive

(if one of the bottles should happen to fall . . .)

the chosen focus tortured true
between a homeless woman lying frozen
on the avenue
and a flying horse or legs to carry you or race
into the hungers of a problematic
new embrace

(. . . 91 bottles of beer on the wall)

I understand the comfortable temptation of the dead:
I turn my back against the grave
and kiss again the risk of what I have
instead

Poem about Process and Progress

For Haruko

Hey Baby you betta
hurry it up!
Because
since you went totally
off
I seen a full moon
I seen a half moon
I seen a quarter moon
I seen no moon whatsoever!

I seen a equinox
I seen a solstice
I seen Mars and Venus on a line
I seen a mess a fickle stars
and lately
I seen this new kind a luva
on an' off the telephone
who like to talk to me
all the time

real nice

Focus in Real Time

Poem for Margaret who passed the California bar!

A bowl of rice
          as food
          as politics
          or metaphor
          as something valuable and good
          or something common to consume/exploit/ignore

Who grew these grains
Who owned the land
Who harvested the crop
Who converted these soft particles to money
Who kept the cash
Who shipped the consequences of the cash
Who else was going to eat the rice
Who else was going to convert the rice to cash

Who would design the flowers for the outside of the bowl
Who would hold the bowl between her hands
Who would give the bowl away
Who could share the rice
Who could fill that bowl with rice how many times a day
          how many times a week
Who would adore the hands that held the bowl that held the rice
Who would adore the look the smell the steam of boiled rice
          in a bowl

Who will analyze the cash the rice becomes
Who will sit beside the bowl or fight for rice
Who will write about the hands that hold the bowl
Who will want to own the land
          A bowl of rice

It's Hard to Keep a Clean Shirt Clean

Poem for Sriram Shamasunder
And All of Poetry for the People

It's a sunlit morning
with jasmine blooming
easily
and a drove of robin redbreasts
diving into the ivy covering
what used to be
a backyard fence
or doves shoving aside
the birch tree leaves
when
a young man walks among
the flowers
to my doorway
where he knocks
then stands still
brilliant in a clean white shirt

He lifts a soft fist
to that door
and knocks again

He's come to say this
was or that
was
not
and what's
anyone of us to do
about what's done
what's past

but prickling salt to sting
our eyes

What's anyone of us to do
about what's done

And 7-month-old Bingo
puppy leaps
and hits
that clean white shirt
with muddy paw
prints here
and here and there

And what's anyone of us to do
about what's done
I say I'll wash the shirt
no problem
two times through
the delicate blue cycle
of an old machine
the shirt spins in the soapy
suds and spins in rinse
and spins
and spins out dry

not clean

still marked by accidents
by energy of whatever serious or trifling cause
the shirt stays dirty
from that puppy's paws

I take that fine white shirt
from India

the threads as soft as baby
fingers weaving them
together
and I wash that shirt
between
between the knuckles of my own
two hands
I scrub and rub that shirt
to take the dirty
markings
out

At the pocket
and around the shoulder seam
and on both sleeves
the dirt the paw
prints tantalize my soap
my water my sweat
equity
invested in the restoration
of a clean white shirt

And on the eleventh try
I see no more
no anything unfortunate
no dirt

I hold the limp fine
cloth
between the faucet stream
of water as transparent
as a wish the moon stayed out
all day

How small it has become!
That clean white shirt!
How delicate!
How slight!
How like a soft fist knocking on my door!
And now I hang the shirt
to dry
as slowly as it needs
the air
to work its way
with everything

It's clean.
A clean white shirt
nobody wanted to spoil
or soil
that shirt
much cleaner now but also
not the same
as the first before that shirt
got hit got hurt
not perfect
anymore
just beautiful

a clean white shirt

It's hard to keep a clean shirt clean.

[·]

Last Poem for a Little While

1

Thanksgiving 1969
Dear God I thank you for the problems that are mine
and evidently mine alone

By mine I mean just ours
crooked perishable blue like blood
problems yielding to no powers
we can muster we can only starve or stud
the sky the soil the stomach of the human hewn

2

(I am in this crazy room
where people all over the place
look at people all over the place.
For instance Emperors in Bronze Black Face
Or Buddha Bodhisattva sandstone trickled old and dirty
        into inexpensive, public space.)

Insanity goes back a long time I suppose.
An alien religion strikes me lightly
And I wonder if it shows
then how?

3

Immediately prior to the messed-up statues that inspire
monographs and fake mistakes
the Greco-Roman paraplegic tricks
the permanently unbent knee
that indoor amphitheater that celebrates the amputee—

Immediately prior to the messed-up statues
just before the lucratively mutilated choir
of worthless lying recollection

There the aged sit and sleep;
for them museum histories spread too far too deep
for actual exploration

(aged men and women) sit and sleep
before the costly exhibition can begin

to tire what remains of life.

4

If love and sex were easier
we would choose something else
to suffer.

5

Holidays do loosen up the holocaust
the memories (sting tides) of rain and refuge
patterns hurt across the stranger city
holidays do loosen up the holocaust
They liberate the stolen totem tongue

The cripples fill the temple
palace entertainment under glass
the cripples crutching near the columns swayed
by plastic wrap
disfiguring haven halls or veils the void
impromptu void
where formerly
Egyptian sarcasucker or more recently

where European painting
turns out nothing
no one
I have ever known.

These environments these
artifacts facsimiles these
metaphors these
earrings vase that sword
none of it
none of it
is somehow what I own.

6

Symbols like the bridge.
Like bridges generally.
Today a flag a red and white and blue new flag
confused the symbols in confusion
bridge over the river
flag over the bridge
The flag hung like a loincloth flicked in drag.

7

Can't cross that bridge. You listen
things is pretty bad
you want to reach New Jersey
got to underslide the lying spangled banner.
Bad enough New Jersey.
Now Songmy.
Songmy. A sorry song. Songmy.
The massacre of sorrow songs.
Songmy. Songmy. Vietnam.
Goddamn. Vietnam.

I would go pray about the bridge.
I would go pray a sorrow Songmy song.
But last time I looked the American flag was flying
from the center of the crucifix.

8

"Well, where you want to go?"
he asks. "I don't know. It's a long
walk to the subway."
"Well," he says, "there's nothing at home."
"That's a sure thing," she answers.
"That's a sure thing: Nothing's at home."

9

Please pass the dark meat.
Turkey's one thing I can eat
and eat.
eeney eeney meeney mo
It's hard to know
whether I should head into
a movie
or take the highway to the airport.
Pass the salt.
Pass the white meat.
Pass the massacre.
o eeney eeney myney mo.
How bad was it, exactly?
What's your evidence?
Songmy o my sorrow
eeney meeney myney mo
Please pass the ham.
I want to show
Vietnam how we give thanks

around here.
Pass the ham.
And wipe your fingers on the flag.

10

Hang my haven
Jesus Christ
is temporarily off
the wall.

11

American existence twists
you finally
into a separatist.

12

I am spiders
on the ceiling of a shadow.

13

Daumier was not mistaken.
Old people sleep with their mouths open
and their hands closed flat
like an empty wallet.

So do I.

To Be Continued:

The partial mastectomy took a long time to execute
And left a huge raggedy scar
Healing from that partial mastectomy took even longer
And devolved into a psychological chasm 2 times the depth
And breadth of the physical scar from the mastectomy that
    was raggedy
And huge
Metastatic reactivation of the breast cancer requiring partial
    mastectomy
That left a huge raggedy scar in the first place now pounds
To pieces
A wound fifty times more implacable and more intractable
Than the psychological chasm produced by the healing process
That was twice as enormously damaging as the surgery
Which left a huge raggedy scar

And so I go
on

Song of the Law Abiding Citizen

so hot so hot so hot so what
so hot so what so hot so hot

They made a mistake
I got more than I usually take
I got food stamps food stamps I got
so many stamps in the mail
I thought maybe I should put them on sale
How lucky I am
I got food stamps: Hot damn!
I made up my mind
to be decent and kind
to let my upright character shine
I sent 10,000 food stamps
back to the President (and his beautiful wife)
and I can't pay the rent
but I sent 10,000 food stamps
back to the President (and his beautiful wife)
how lucky I am
hot damn
They made a mistake
for Chrissake
And I gave it away to the President
I thought that was legal I thought that was kind
and I can't pay the rent
but I sent 10,000 food stamps
back back back to the President

so hot so hot so hot so what
so hot so what so hot so hot

Trucks cruisin' down the avenue
carrying nuclear garbage right next to you
and it's legal
it's radioaction ridin' like a regal
load of jewels
past the bars the cruel
school house and the church and if
the trucks wipeout or crash
or even lurch too hard around a corner
we will just be goners
and it's legal
it's radioaction ridin' regal
through the skittery city street
and don't be jittery
because it's legal
radioaction ridin' the road
Avenue A Avenue B Avenue C Avenue D
Avenue of the Americas

so hot so hot so hot so what
so hot so what so hot so hot
so hot so hot so hot so what

Letter to the Local Police

Dear Sirs:

I have been enjoying the law and order of our
community throughout the past three months since
my wife and I, our two cats, and miscellaneous
photographs of the six grandchildren belonging to
our previous neighbors (with whom we were very
close) arrived in Saratoga Springs which is clearly
prospering under your custody

Indeed, until yesterday afternoon and despite my
vigilant casting about, I have been unable to discover
a single instance of reasons for public-spirited concern,
much less complaint

You may easily appreciate, then, how it is that
I write to your office, at this date, with utmost
regret for the lamentable circumstances that force
my hand

Speaking directly to the issue of the moment:

I have encountered a regular profusion of certain
unidentified roses, growing to no discernible purpose,
and according to no perceptible control, approximately
one quarter mile west of the Northway, on the southern
side

To be specific, there are practically thousands of
the aforementioned abiding in perpetual near riot
of wild behavior, indiscriminate coloring, and only
the Good Lord Himself can say what diverse soliciting
of promiscuous cross-fertilization

As I say, these roses, no matter what the apparent
background, training, tropistic tendencies, age,
or color, do not demonstrate the least inclination
toward categorization, specified allegiance, resolute
preference, consideration of the needs of others, or
any other minimal traits of decency

May I point out that I did not assiduously seek out
this colony, as it were, and that these certain
unidentified roses remain open to viewing even by
children, with or without suitable supervision

(My wife asks me to append a note as regards the
seasonal but nevertheless seriously licentious
phenomenon of honeysuckle under the moon that one may
apprehend at the corner of Nelson and Main

However, I have recommended that she undertake direct
correspondence with you, as regards this: yet
another civic disturbance in our midst)

I am confident that you will devise and pursue
appropriate legal response to the roses in question
If I may aid your efforts in this respect, please
do not hesitate to call me into consultation

                              Respectfully yours,

Owed to Eminem

I'm the Slim Lady the real Slim Lady
the real Slim Lady just a little ole lady
uh-huh
uh-huh
I'm Slim Lady the real Slim Lady
all them other age ladies
just tryin to page me
but I'm Slim Lady the real Slim Lady
and I will
stand up
I will stand up

I assume that you fume while the
      dollar bills bloom
and you magnify scum while the
      critics stay mum
and you anguish and languish runnin
      straight to the bank
and you scheme and you team with
      false balls so you rank
at the top and you pop like the jury the
      victim
the judge
but the ghetto don't trip to the light
      stuff you flip
on the chain saw you skip
with
the rope and the knives and that bunk
      about tying who up like a punk in the
back of the trunk
or that dope about mothers and wives

       give you worse than a funeral hearse
fulla
hickies and hives
you fudge
where you come from or whether you
       mean it
the shit you can't make without
       sycophants see'n it
but nobody's dumb
enough to believe that you grieve
       because folks
can't conceive that you more than a
       moron
or why would you whore on
the hole in your soul?

At this stage of my rage
I'm a sage so I know how you blow
to the left then the right and you maim
every Columbine game about "No!
       Cuz he's white!"

But I am that I am
and I don't give a damn
and you mess with my jam
and I'll kill you
I will!

And if you insist listenin close for a dis
then you missin more than the gist in
       this
because
I gotcha pose by the nose

I hear how you laugh and cut corners
		in half
And I see you wigglin a line that's not
		flat
while you screwin around with more
		than all that

But I am that I am
and I don't give a damn
and you mess with my jam
and I'll kill you
I will!

Don't tell me you pissed or who's
		slashin whose wrists
or pretend about risks
to a blond millionaire
with a bodyguard crew that prey
behind shades and that pay
to get laid—What?
What's that about fair?

I'm not through with you!

I'm the bitch in the bedroom the
		faggot
you chump I'm the nigga for real so get
		ready to deal
I'm tired of wiggas that whine as they
		squeal
about bitches and faggots and little
		girls too!
I'm a Arab I'm a Muslim I'm a
		Orthodox Jew!

I'm the bitch come to take you
I'm the faggot to fake you
outta the closet
outta the closet
fulla the slime you deposit
for fun

rhyme and run
you the number one
phony-ass gun

Oh! I am that I am
and I don't give a damn
and you mess with my jam
and I'll kill you
I will!

(Hey, Shady
you know what I'm sayin
I'm just playin!
You know I love you!)

Sincerely,

Slim Lady

The Bombing of Baghdad

1

began and did not terminate for 42 days
and 42 nights relentless minute after minute
more than 110,000 times
we bombed Iraq we bombed Baghdad
we bombed Basra/we bombed military
installations we bombed the National Museum
we bombed schools we bombed air raid
shelters we bombed water we bombed
electricity we bombed hospitals we
bombed streets we bombed highways
we bombed everything that moved/we
bombed everything that did not move we
bombed Baghdad
a city of 5.5 million human beings
we bombed radio towers we bombed
telephone poles we bombed mosques
we bombed runways we bombed tanks
we bombed trucks we bombed cars we bombed bridges
we bombed the darkness we bombed
the sunlight we bombed them and we
bombed them and we cluster bombed the citizens
of Iraq and we sulfur bombed the citizens of Iraq
and we napalm bombed the citizens of Iraq and we
complemented these bombings/these "sorties" with
Tomahawk cruise missiles which we shot
repeatedly by the thousands upon thousands
into Iraq
(you understand an Iraqi Scud missile
is *quote* militarily insignificant *unquote* and we
do not mess around with insignificant)

so we used cruise missiles repeatedly
we fired them into Iraq
And I am not pleased
I am not very pleased
None of this fits into my notion of "things going very well"

2

The bombing of Baghdad
did not obliterate the distance or the time
between my body and the breath
of my beloved

3

This was Custer's Next-To-Last Stand
I hear Crazy Horse singing as he dies
I dedicate myself to learn that song
I hear that music in the moaning of the Arab world

4

Custer got accustomed to just doing his job
Pushing westward into glory
Making promises
Searching for the savages/their fragile
temporary settlements
for raising children/dancing down the rain/and praying
for the mercy of a herd of buffalo
Custer/he pursued these savages
He attacked at dawn
He murdered the men/murdered the boys
He captured the women and converted
them (I'm sure)
to his religion

Oh, how gently did he bid his darling fiancée
farewell!
How sweet the gaze her eyes bestowed upon her warrior!
Loaded with guns and gunpowder he embraced
the guts and gore of manifest white destiny
He pushed westward
to annihilate the savages
("Attack at dawn!")
and seize their territories
    seize their women
    seize their natural wealth

5

And I am cheering for the arrows
and the braves

6

And all who believed some must die
they were already dead
And all who believe only they possess
human being and therefore human rights
they no longer stood among the possibly humane
And all who believed that retaliation/revenge/defense
derive from God-given prerogatives of white men
And all who believed that waging war is anything
        besides terrorist activity in the first
        place and in the last
And all who believed that F-15s/F-16s/"Apache"
        helicopters/
B-52 bombers/smart bombs/dumb bombs/napalm/artillery/
battleships/nuclear warheads amount to anything other
than terrorist tools of a terrorist undertaking

And all who believed that holocaust means something
        that only happens to white people
And all who believed that Desert Storm
        signified anything besides the delivery of an American
        holocaust against the peoples of the Middle East
All who believed these things
they were already dead
They no longer stood among the possibly humane

And this is for Crazy Horse singing as he dies
because I live inside his grave
And this is for the victims of the bombing of Baghdad
because the enemy traveled from my house
        to blast your homeland
        into pieces of children
        and pieces of sand

And in the aftermath of carnage
perpetrated in my name
how should I dare to offer you my hand
how shall I negotiate the implications
        of my shame?

My heart cannot confront
this death without relief
My soul will not control
this leaking of my grief

And this is for Crazy Horse singing as he dies
And here is my song of the living
who must sing against the dying
sing to join the living
with the dead

Poem for Nana

What will we do
when there is nobody left
to kill?

                    ~

40,000 gallons of oil gushing into
the ocean
But I
sit on top this mountainside above
the Pacific
checking out the flowers
the California poppies orange
as I meet myself in heat
                    I'm wondering
where's the Indians?

                    all this filmstrip territory
                    all this cowboy sagaland:
                    not
                    a single Indian
                    in sight

40,000 gallons gushing up poison
from the deepest seabeds
every hour

40,000 gallons
while
experts international
while
new pollutants

swallow the unfathomable
still:

no Indians

I'm staring hard around me
past the pinks the poppies and the precipice
that let me see the wide Pacific
unsuspecting
even trivial
by virtue of its vast surrender

I am a woman searching for her savagery
even if it's doomed

Where are the Indians?

~

Crow Nose
Little Bear
Slim Girl
Black Elk
Fox Belly

the people of the sacred trees
and rivers precious to the stars that told
old stories to the night

how do we follow after you?

falling
snow before the firelight
and buffalo as brothers
to the man

how do we follow into that?

~

They found her facedown
where she would be dancing
to the shadow drums that humble
birds to silent
    flight

They found her body held
its life dispelled
by ice
my life burns to destroy

Anna Mae Pictou Aquash
slain on The Trail of Broken Treaties
bullet lodged in her brain/hands
and fingertips
dismembered

who won the only peace
that cannot pass
from mouth to mouth

~

Memory should agitate
the pierced bone crack
of one in pushed-back horror
pushed-back pain
as when I call out looking for my face
among the wounded coins
to toss about
or out
entirely

the legends of Geronimo
of Pocahontas
now become a squat
pedestrian cement inside the tomb
of all my trust

as when I feel you isolate
among the hungers of the trees
a trembling
hidden tinder so long unsolicited
by flame

as when I accept my sister dead
when there should be
a fluid holiness
of spirits wrapped around the world
redeemed by women
whispering communion

~

I find my way by following your spine

Your heart indivisible from my real wish
we
compelled the moon into the evening when
you said, "No,
I will not let go
of your hand."

~

Now I am diving for a tide to take me everywhere

Below
the soft Pacific spoils

a purple girdling of the globe
impregnable

~

Last year the South African Minister of Justice
described Anti-Government Disturbances as
Part of a Worldwide Trend toward the
Breakdown of Established Political and Cultural
Orders

~

God knows I hope he's right.

Ghazal at Full Moon

I try to describe how this aching begins or how it began
with an obsolete coin and the obsolete head of an obsolete Indian.

Holding a nickel I beheld a buffalo I beheld the silver face
of a man who might be your father: A dead man: An Indian.

I thought, "Indians pray. Indians dance. But, mostly, Indians do not live.
In the U.S.A.," we said, "the only good Indian is a dead Indian."

Dumb like Christopher Columbus I could not factor out the obvious
denominator: Guatemala/Wisconsin/Jamaica/Colorado: Indian.

Nicaragua and Brazil, Arizona, Illinois, North Dakota, and New Mexico:
The Indigenous: The shining and the shadow of the eye is Indian.

One billion fifty-six, five-hundred-and-thirty-seven-thousand people
breathing in India, Pakistan, Bangladesh: All of them Indian.

Ocho Rios Oklahoma Las Vegas Pearl Lagoon Chicago
Bombay Panjim Liverpool Lahore Comalapa Glasgow: Indian.

From a London pub among the lager louts to Machu Picchu
I am following an irresistible a tenuous and livid profile: Indian.

I find a surging latticework inside the merciless detritus of diaspora.
We go from death to death who see any difference here from Indian.

The voice desiring your tongue transmits from the light of the clouds
     as it can.
Indian Indian Indian   Indian Indian Indian Indian.

Poem to Take Back the Night

What about moonlight
What about watching for the moon above
the tops of trees and standing
still enough to hear the raucous crickets
chittering invisible among the soon lit stones
trick pinpoints of positions even poise
sustained in solitary loss

What about moonlight
What about moonlight

What about watching for the moon
through the windows low enough to let the screams
and curses of the street the gunshots
and the drunken driver screeching tires
and the boom box big beat and the tinkle
bell ice cream truck
inside

What about moonlight
What about moonlight

What about watching for the moon
behind the locked doors and bolted shut bedrooms
and the blind side of venetian blinds and
cowering under the kitchen table and struggling
from the car and wrestling head
down when the surprise when the
stranger when the surprise when the
coach when the surprise when the
priest when the surprise when the
doctor when the surprise when the

family when the surprise when the
lover when the surprise when the
friend when the surprise

lacerates your throat
constricted into no
no more sound

who will whisper
what about moonlight
what about moonlight

What about watching for the moon
so far from where you tremble
where you bleed where you sob
out loud for help or mercy for
a thunderbolt of shame and
retribution where you plead
with God and devils with
the creatures in-between
to push the power key
and set you free
from filth and blasphemy
from everything you never wanted to feel
or see

to set you free

so you could brush your teeth
and comb your hair and maybe
throw on a jacket
or maybe not

you running
curious and so excited and

running and running into the
night
asking only asking

What about the moonlight
What about the moonlight

To Sing a Song of Palestine

For Shula Koenig (Israeli Peace Activist)

All the natural wonders that don't grow there
(Nor tree nor river nor a great plains lifting grain
nor grass nor rooted fruit and
vegetables) forever curse the land
with wildly dreaming schemes
of transformation
military magic
thick accomplishments of blood.

I sing of Israel and Palestine:
The world as neither yours nor mine:
How many different men will fit
themselves how fast
into that place?

A woman's body as the universal
shelter to the demon or the sweet as paradigm
of home that starts and ends with face
to face surrendering to the need
that each of us can feed or take
away
amazing as the space created
by the mothers of our time
—can we behold ourselves
    like that
the ribs the breathing muscles and the fat
of everything desire requires
for its rational abatement?

I write beside the rainy sky

tonight an unexpected an American
cease-fire to the burning day
that worked like war across my
empty throat before I thought to try this way
to say I think we can: I think we can.

First poem from Nicaragua Libre: Teotecacinte

Can you say Teotecacinte?
Can you say it,
Teotecacinte?

Into the dirt she fell
she blew up the shell
fell into the dirt the artillery
shell blew up the girl
crouching near to the well of the little house
with the cool roof thatched on the slant
the little girl of the little house fell
beside the well unfinished for water
when that mortar
shattered the dirt under her barefeet
and scattered pieces of her four
year old anatomy
into the yard dust and up
among the lower branches of a short tree

Can you say it?

That is two and a half inches of her scalp there
with the soft hairs stiffening
in the grass

Teotecacinte
Can you say it,
Teotecacinte?

Can you say it?

Second poem from Nicaragua Libre: war zone

On the night road from El Rama the cows
congregate fully in the middle and you
wait
looking at the cowhide colors bleached
by the high stars above their bodies
big with ribs

At some point you just have to trust
somebody else the soldier
wearing a white shirt the poet
wearing glasses the woman
wearing red shoes
into combat

At dawn the student gave me a caramel
candy and pigs and dogs ran into the streets
as the sky began the gradual
wide burn and towards the top
of a new mountain I saw
the teen-age shadows of two sentries
armed with automatics
checking the horizon
for slow stars

Third poem from Nicaragua Libre: photograph of Managua

The man is not cute.
The man is not ugly.
The man is teaching himself
to read.
He sits in a kitchen chair
under a banana tree.
He holds the newspaper.
He tracks each word with a finger
and opens his mouth to the sound.
Next to the chair the old V-Z rifle
leans at the ready.
His wife chases a baby pig with a homemade
broom and then she chases her daughter running
behind the baby pig.
His neighbor washes up with water from the barrel
after work.
The dirt floor of his house has been swept.
The dirt around the chair where he sits
has been swept.
He has swept the dirt twice.
The dirt is clean.
The dirt is his dirt.
The man is not cute.
The man is not ugly.
The man is teaching himself
to read.

Fourth poem from Nicaragua Libre:
report from the frontier

gone gone gone ghost
gone
both the house of the hard dirt floor and the church
next door
torn apart more raggedy than skeletons
when the bombs hit
leaving a patch of her hair on a piece of her scalp
like bird's nest
in the dark yard still lit by flowers

I found
the family trench empty
the pails of rainwater standing full
a soldier whistling while thunder invaded
the afternoon
shards
shreds
one electric bulb split by bullets
dead hanging plants
two Sandinistas riding donkeys
a child sucking a mango
many dogs lost
five seconds left above the speechless
tobacco fields
like a wooden bridge you wouldn't
trust
with the weight of a cat

A Song of Sojourner Truth

Dedicated to Bernice Reagon

The trolley cars was rollin and the passengers all white
when Sojourner just decided it was time to take a seat
The trolley cars was rollin and the passengers all white
When Sojourner decided it was time to take a seat
It was time she felt to rest awhile and ease up
on her feet
So Sojourner put her hand out
tried to flag the trolley down
So Sojourner put her hand out
for the trolley crossin town
And the driver did not see her
the conductor would not stop
But Sojourner yelled, "It's me!"
And put her body on the track
"It's me!" she yelled, "And yes,
I walked here but I ain' walkin back!"
The trolley car conductor and the driver was afraid
to roll right over her and leave her lying dead
So they opened up the car and Sojourner took a seat
So Sojourner sat to rest awhile and eased up on her feet

    REFRAIN:

Sojourner had to be just crazy
tellin all that kinda truth
I say she musta been plain crazy
plus they say she was uncouth
talkin loud to any crowd
talkin bad insteada sad
She just had to be plain crazy
talkin all that kinda truth

PASSION, 1980   69

If she had somewhere to go she said
I'll ride
If she had somewhere to go she said
I'll ride
jim crow or no
she said *I'll go*
just like the lady
that she was in all the knowing darkness
of her pride
she said *I'll ride*
she said *I'll talk*
she said *A Righteous Mouth*
ain' nothin you should hide
she said she'd ride
just like the lady
that she was in all the knowing darkness
of her pride
she said *I'll ride*

They said she's Black and ugly and they said she's
really rough
They said if you treat her like a dog
well that'll be plenty good enough
And Sojourner said
I'll ride
And Sojourner said
I'll go
I'm a woman and this hell has made me tough
(Thank God)
This hell has made me tough
I'm a strong Black woman
and Thank God!

REFRAIN:

Sojourner had to be just crazy
tellin all that kinda truth
I say she musta been plain crazy
plus they say she was uncouth
talkin loud to any crowd
talkin bad insteada sad
She just had to be plain crazy
talkin all that kinda truth

My Sadness Sits Around Me

My sadness sits around me
       not on haunches not in any
       placement near a move
and the tired roll-on
of a boredom without grief

If there were war
I would watch the hunting
I would chase the dogs
and blow the horn
because blood is commonplace

As I walk in peace
       unencountered unmolested
       unimpinging unbelieving unrevealing
       undesired under every O
My sadness sits around me

[·]

Getting Down to Get Over

Dedicated to my mother

1

MOMMA MOMMA MOMMA
momma momma
mammy
nanny
granny
woman
mistress
sista

luv

blackgirl
slavegirl

gal

honeychile
sweetstuff
sugar
sweetheart
baby
Baby Baby

MOMMA MOMMA
Black Momma
Black bitch
Black pussy
piecea tail

nice piecea ass

hey daddy! hey
bro!
we walk together (an')
talk together (an')
dance and *do*
(together)
dance and do/hey!
daddy!
bro!
hey!
nina nikki nonni nommo nommo
momma Black
Momma

Black Woman
Black
Female Head of Household
Black Matriarchal Matriarchy
Black Statistical
Lowlife Lowlevel Lowdown
Lowdown and *up*
to be Low-down
Black Statistical
Low Factor
Factotum
Factitious Fictitious
Figment Figuring in Lowdown Lyin
Annual Reports

Black Woman/Black
Hallelujah Saintly
patient

smilin
humble
givin thanks
for
Annual Reports and
Monthly Dole
and
Friday night
and
(*good* God!)
Monday mornin: Black and Female
martyr masochist
(A BIG WHITE LIE)
Momma Momma

What does Mothafuckin mean?
WHO'S THE MOTHAFUCKA
FUCKED MY MOMMA
messed yours over
and right now
be trippin on my starveblack
female soul
a macktruck
mothafuck
the first primordial
the paradig/digmatic
dogmatistic mothafucka who
is he?
hey!
momma momma

dry eyes on the
shy/dark/hidden/cryin Black
face

of the loneliness
the rape
the brokeup mailbox
an' no western union roses
come inside the kitchen
and no poem
take you through the whole night
and no big
Black
burly
hand
be holdin yours
to have to hold onto
no
big Black burly hand
no nommo
no Black prince
come riding from the darkness
on a beautiful black horse
no bro
no daddy

"I was sixteen when I met my father.
In a bar.
In Baltimore.
He told me who he was
and what he does.
Paid for the drinks.
I looked.
I listened.
And I left him.
It was civil
perfectly
and absolute bull

shit.
The drinks was leakin waterweak
and never got down to my knees."

hey daddy
what they been and done to you
and what you been and done
to me
to momma
momma momma
hey
sugar daddy
big daddy
sweet daddy
Black Daddy
The Original Father Divine
the everlovin
deep
tall
bad
buck
jive
cold
strut
bop
split
tight
loose
close
hot
hot
hot
sweet SWEET DADDY
WHERE YOU BEEN AND

WHEN YOU COMIN BACK TO ME
HEY
WHEN YOU COMIN BACK
TO MOMMA
momma momma

And Suppose He Finally Say
"Look, Baby.
I Loves Me Some
Everything about You.
Let Me Be Your Man."
That reach around the hurtin
like a dream.
And I ain' never wakin up
from that one.
momma momma
momma momma

2

Consider the Queen

hand on her hip
sweat restin from
the corn/bean/greens' field
steamy under the pale/sly
suffocatin sky

Consider the Queen

she fix the cufflinks
on his Sunday shirt
and fry some chicken
bake some cake
and tell the family

"Never mind about the bossman
don' know how a human
bein spozed to act. Jus'
never mind about him.
Wash your face.
Sit down. And let
the good Lord bless this table."

Consider the Queen

her babies pullin at the nipples
pullin at the momma milk

the infant fingers gingerly
approach caress the
soft/Black/swollen/momma breast

and there
inside the mommasoft
life-spillin treasure chest
the heart
breaks

rage by grief by sorrow
weary weary
breaks
breaks quiet
silently
the weary sorrow
quiet now the furious
the adamant the broken
busted beaten down and beaten up
the beaten beaten beaten
weary heart beats
tender-steady

and the babies suck/
the seed of blood
and love glows at the
soft/Black/swollen momma breast

Consider the Queen

she works when she works
in the laundry *in jail*
in the school house *in jail*
in the office *in jail*
on the soap box *in jail*
on the desk
on the floor
on the street
on the line
at the door
lookin fine
at the head of the line
steppin sharp from behind
in the light
with a song
wearing boots
or a belt
and a gun
drinkin wine when it's time
when the long week is done
but she works when she works
in the laundry in jail
she works when she works

Consider the Queen

she sleeps when she sleeps

with the king in the kingdom
she
sleeps when she sleeps
with the wall
with whatever it is who happens
to call
with me and with you
(to survive you make
do/you explore more and more)
so she sleeps when she sleeps
a really deep sleep

Consider the Queen

a full/Black/glorious/a purple rose
aroused by the tiger breathin
beside her
a shell with the moanin
of ages inside her
a hungry one feedin the folk
what they need

Consider the Queen.

   3

Blackman
let that white girl go
She know what you ought to know.
(By now.)

   4

MOMMA MOMMA
momma momma

family face
face of the family alive
momma
mammy
momma
woman
sista
baby
luv

the house on fire/
poison waters/
earthquake/
and the air a nightmare/
turn
turn
turn around the
national gross product
growin
really gross/turn
turn
turn the pestilence away
the miserable killers
and Canarsie
Alabama
people beggin to be people
warfare on the welfare
of the folk/
hey
turn
turn away
the trickbag university/the
trickbag propaganda/
trickbag

tricklins of prosperity/of
pseudo-"status"
lynchtree necklace
on the strong
round
neck of you
my momma
momma momma
turn away
the f.b.i./the state police/the cops/
the/everyone of the
infest/incestuous investigators
into you
and Daddy/into us
hey
turn
my mother
turn
the face of history
to your own
and please be smilin
if you can
be smilin
at the family

momma momma

let the funky forecast
be the last
one we will ever
want to listen to

And Daddy see
the stars fall down

and burn a light
into the singin
darkness of your eyes
my Daddy
my Blackman
you take my body in
your arms/you use
the oil of coconuts/of trees and
flowers/fish and new fruits
from the new world
to enflame me in this otherwise
cold place
please

meanwhile
momma
momma momma
teach me how to kiss
the king within the kingdom
teach me how to t.c.b./to make do
and be
like you
teach me to survive my
momma
teach me how to hold a new life
momma
help me
turn the face of history
to your face.

Case in Point

A friend of mine who raised six daughters and
who never wrote what she regards as serious
until she
was fifty-three
tells me there is no silence peculiar
to the female

I have decided I have something to say
about female silence: so to speak
these are my 2¢ on the subject:
2 weeks ago I was raped for the second
time in my life the first occasion
being a whiteman and the most recent
situation being a blackman actually
head of the local NAACP

Today is 2 weeks after the fact
of that man straddling
his knees either side of my chest
his hairy arm and powerful left hand
forcing my arms and my hands over my head
flat to the pillow while he rammed
what he described as his quote big dick
unquote into my mouth
and shouted out: "D'ya want to swallow
my big dick; well, do ya?"

He was being rhetorical.
My silence was peculiar
to the female.

Notes towards Home

My born on 99th Street uncle when he went to Canada
used to wash and polish the car long before coffee
every morning outside his room in the motel
"Because," he said, "that way they thought I lived
around there; you ever hear of a perfectly clean car
traveling all the way from Brooklyn to Quebec?"

My mother left the barefoot roads of St. Mary's
in Jamaica for the States where she wore
stockings even in a heat wave and repeatedly
advised me never to wear tacky underwear
"That way," she said, "if you have an accident
when they take you to a hospital they'll know you
come from a home."

After singing God Bless America Kate Smith
bellowed the willies out of Bless This House O
Lord We Pray/Make It Safe By Night and Day
but my cousin meant Lord keep June
and her Boris Karloff imitations out of the hall
and my mother meant Lord keep my husband out
of my way and I remember I used to mean Lord
just pretty please get me out of here!

But everybody needs a home
so at least you have someplace to leave
which is where most other folks will say
you must be coming from

Moving towards Home

"Where is Abu Fadi," she wailed.
"Who will bring me my loved one?"

The New York Times, *9/20/82*

I do not wish to speak about the bulldozer and the
red dirt
not quite covering all of the arms and legs
Nor do I wish to speak about the nightlong screams
that reached
the observation posts where soldiers lounged about
Nor do I wish to speak about the woman who shoved
her baby
into the stranger's hands before she was led away
Nor do I wish to speak about the father whose sons
were shot
through the head while they slit his own throat before
the eyes
of his wife
Nor do I wish to speak about the army that lit continuous
flares into the darkness so that the others could see
the backs of their victims lined against the wall
Nor do I wish to speak about the piled up bodies and
the stench
that will not float
Nor do I wish to speak about the nurse again and
again raped
before they murdered her on the hospital floor
Nor do I wish to speak about the rattling bullets that
did not
halt on that keening trajectory
Nor do I wish to speak about the pounding on the

doors and
the breaking of windows and the hauling of families into
the world of the dead
I do not wish to speak about the bulldozer and the
red dirt
not quite covering all of the arms and legs
because I do not wish to speak about unspeakable events
that must follow from those who dare
"to purify" a people
those who dare
"to exterminate" a people
those who dare
to describe human beings as "beasts with two legs"
those who dare
"to mop up"
"to tighten the noose"
"to step up the military pressure"
"to ring around" civilian streets with tanks
those who dare
to close the universities
to abolish the press
to kill the elected representatives
of the people who refuse to be purified
those are the ones from whom we must redeem
the words of our beginning

because I need to speak about home
I need to speak about living room
where the land is not bullied and beaten to
a tombstone
I need to speak about living room
where the talk will take place in my language
I need to speak about living room
where my children will grow without horror

I need to speak about living room where the men
of my family between the ages of six and sixty-five
are not
marched into a roundup that leads to the grave
I need to talk about living room
where I can sit without grief without wailing aloud
for my loved ones
where I must not ask where is Abu Fadi
because he will be there beside me
I need to talk about living room
because I need to talk about home

I was born a Black woman
and now
I am become a Palestinian
against the relentless laughter of evil
there is less and less living room
and where are my loved ones?

It is time to make our way home.

A Short Note to My Very Critical and Well-Beloved Friends and Comrades

First they said I was too light
Then they said I was too dark
Then they said I was too different
Then they said I was too much the same
Then they said I was too young
Then they said I was too old
Then they said I was too interracial
Then they said I was too much a nationalist
Then they said I was too silly
Then they said I was too angry
Then they said I was too idealistic
Then they said I was too confusing altogether:
Make up your mind! They said. Are you militant
or sweet? Are you vegetarian or meat? Are you straight
or are you gay?

And I said, Hey! It's not about *my* mind.

Okay "Negroes"

Okay "Negroes"
American Negroes
looking for milk
crying out loud
in the nursery of freedomland:
the rides are rough.
Tell me where you got that image
of a male white mammy.
God is vague and he don't take no sides.
You think clean fingernails crossed legs a smile
shined shoes
a crucifix around your neck
good manners
no more noise
you think who's gonna give you something?

Come a little closer.
Where you from?

What Would I Do White?

What would I do white?
What would I do clearly full
of not exactly beans nor
pearls my nose a manicure
my eyes a picture of your wall?

I would disturb the streets by
passing by so pretty kids
on stolen petty cash would look
at me like foreign
writing in the sky

I would forget my furs on any chair.
I would ignore the doormen at the knob
the social sanskrit of my life
unwilling to disclose my cosmetology,
I would forget.

Over my wine I would acquire
I would inspire big returns to equity
the equity of capital I am
accustomed to accept

like wintertime.

I would do nothing.
That would be enough.

May 27, 1971: No Poem

blood stains Union Street in Mississippi

so now there will be
another investigation to see
whether or not
the murder of the running young girl
by drunken whiteboys
was
a Federal offense
                    "of some kind"

there are no details to her early death
her
high school graduation
glory
yellow dress
branded
new the rolled-up
clean
diploma
certifying ready
certifying aim
certifying shot
by bathtub whiskey hatred by
a bloody .22 let loose
at her life

Joetha Collier she was
killed

at eighteen only
daughter

born to Mr. and Mrs. Love
the family
Black love wracked
by outside hogstyle hatred
on the bullet fly

Joetha Collier she was
young and she
was Black and she was
she was
she was

and

blood stains Union Street in Mississippi

Grand Army Plaza

For Ethelbert

Why would anybody build a monument to civil war?

The tall man and myself tonight
we will not sleep together
we may not
either one of us
sleep
in any case
the differential between friend and lover
is a problem
definitions curse
as *nowadays we're friends*
or
we were lovers once
while
overarching the fastidious the starlit
dust
that softens space between us
is the history that bleeds
through shirt and blouse
alike

the stain of skin on stone

But on this hard ground curved by memories
of union and disunion and of brothers dead
by the familiar hand
how do we face to face a man
a woman
interpenetrated

free
and reaching still toward the kiss that will
not suffocate?

We are not survivors of a civil war

We survive our love
because we go on

loving

On Moral Leadership as a Political Dilemma

Watergate, 1973

I don't know why but
I cannot tell a lie

I chopped down the cherry tree
I did
I did that
yessirree
I chopped down the cherry tree

and to tell you the truth
see
that was only in the morning

which left a whole day and part
of an evening (until suppertime)
to continue doing what I like to do
about cherry trees

which is

to chop them down

then pick the cherries
and roll them into a cherry-pie circle
and then
stomp the cherries
stomp them
jumping up and down

hard and heavy
jumping up to stomp them

so the flesh leaks and the juice
runs loose
and then I get to pick at the pits
or else I pick up the cherry pits
(depending on my mood)
and then
I fill my mouth completely full
of cherry pits
and run over to the river
the Potomac
where I spit
the cherry pits
47 to 65 cherry pits spit
into the Potomac
at one spit

and to tell you the truth some more
if I ever see a cherry tree
standing around no matter where
and here let me please be perfectly clear
no matter where
I see a cherry tree
standing around
even if it belongs to a middle-American of
moderate means with a two-car family
that is falling apart in a respectable
civilized
falling apart
mind-your-manners manner

even then
or even if you happen to be
corporate rich or
unspeakably poor or famous

or fashionably thin or comfortably fat
or even as peculiar as misguided as
a Democrat

or even a Democrat

even then
see
if you have a cherry tree
and I see it
I will chop that cherry tree down
stomp the cherries
fill my mouth completely with the pits to
spit them into the Potomac
and I don't know why
it is
that I cannot tell a lie

but that's the truth.

Home: January 29, 1984

I can tell
because the ashtray was cleaned out
because the downstairs coconut is still full of milk
because actually nothing was left
except two shells hinged together pretty tough
at the joint
I can tell
because the in-house music now includes
the lying down look of gold and your shoulders
because there is no more noise in my head
because one room two hallways two flights of stairs
and the rest of northamerica remain
to be seen in this movie about why
I am trying to write this poem

                        not a letter
                        not a proclamation
                        not a history

I am trying to write this poem
because I can tell
because it's way after midnight and so what
I can tell
eyes open or shut
I can tell
George Washington did not sleep
here
I can tell
it was you
I can tell
it really was
you

Notes on the Peanut

For the Poet David Henderson

Hi there. My name is George
Washington
Carver.
If you will bear with me
for a few minutes I
will share with you
a few
of the 30,117 uses to which
the lowly peanut has been put
by me
since yesterday afternoon.
If you will look at my feet you will notice
my sensible shoelaces made from unadulterated
peanut leaf composition that is biodegradable
in the extreme.
To your left you can observe the lovely Renoir
masterpiece reproduction that I have cleverly
pieced together from several million peanut
shell chips painted painstakingly so as to
accurately represent the colors of the original!
Overhead you will spot a squadron of Peanut B-52
Bombers flying due west.
I would extend my hands to greet you
at this time
except for the fact that I am holding a reserve
supply of high energy dry roasted peanuts
guaranteed to accelerate protein assimilation
precisely documented by my pocket peanut calculator;

May I ask when did you last contemplate the relationship
between the expanding peanut products industry
and the development of post-Marxian economic theory
which (Let me emphasize) need not exclude moral attrition
of prepuberty
polymorphic
prehensible skills within the population age sectors
of 8 to 15?
I hope you will excuse me if I appear to be staring at you
through these functional yet high fashion and prescriptive
peanut contact lenses providing for the most
minute observation of your physical response to all of this
ultimately nutritional information.
Peanut butter peanut soap peanut margarine peanut
brick houses and house and field peanuts per se well
illustrate the diversified
potential of this lowly leguminous plant
to which you may correctly refer
also
as the goober the pindar the groundnut
and ground pea/let me
interrupt to take your name down on my
pocket peanut writing pad complete with matching
peanut pencil that only 3 or 4
chewing motions of the jaws will sharpen
into pyrotechnical utility
and no sweat.
Please:
Speak right into the peanut!

Your name?

Poem about Police Violence

Tell me something
what you think would happen if
everytime they kill a black boy
then we kill a cop
everytime they kill a black man
then we kill a cop

you think the accident rate would lower
subsequently?

sometimes the feeling like amaze me baby
comes back to my mouth and I am quiet
like Olympian pools from the running the
mountainous snows under the sun

sometimes thinking about the 12th House of the Cosmos
or the way your ear ensnares the tip
of my tongue or signs that I have never seen
like DANGER WOMEN WORKING

I lose consciousness of ugly bestial rabid
and repetitive affront as when they tell me
18 cops in order to subdue one man
18 strangled him to death in the ensuing scuffle (don't
you idolize the diction of the powerful: *subdue* and
scuffle my oh my) and that the murder
that the killing of Arthur Miller on a Brooklyn
street was just a "justifiable accident" again
(again)

People been having accidents all over the globe
so long like that I reckon that the only

suitable insurance is a gun
I'm saying war is not to understand or rerun
war is to be fought and won

sometimes the feeling like amaze me baby
blots it out/the bestial but
not too often

tell me something
what you think would happen if
everytime they kill a black boy
then we kill a cop
everytime they kill a black man
then we kill a cop

you think the accident rate would lower
subsequently?

On the Black Family

we making love real
they mining the rivers

we been going without trees and going
without please and growing on—
on make-dos and breakthroughs to baby
makes three's a family
ole Charlie knows nothing
about out there
where
he burning the leaves and firing the earth
and killing and killing

we been raising the children
to hold us some love for tomorrows
that show how we won our own wars
just to come in the night
Black and Loving
Man and Woman
definitely in despite
of
all the hurdles that the murdering
masterminds threw up to stop
the comings of
Black Love

we came
we came and we come in a glory of darkness
around the true reasons for sharing
our dark and our beautiful
name
that we give to our dark and our beautiful

daughters and sons
who must make the same struggle
to love

and must win

against the tyrannical soldierly sins
of the ones who beatify plastic and steel
and who fly themselves high on the failure to feel

    —they mining the rivers
    we making love real

Racial Profile #3

A boat in the water
Not so big
Sails full
Or buckling
Or drenched
Or furled up tight and tied
To a torn-up masthead

A boat in the water
Not so big
A boat

Still in the water

1978

The woman who left the house this morning
more or less on her way to Mississippi more
or less through Virginia in order to pack and get back to
New York on her way to the People's Republic of
Angola
was
stopped in Washington D.C. by an undercover
agent for the C.I.A. offering to help her with
her bags

The woman who came to the house tonight with
her boy baby Ché on the way to Philly
for a showdown with Customs that wants to deport both
of them
to Venezuela because Ché's
father months ago ducked out
entirely
she
just offered to make me chickweed tea
for my runny nose cold

"You know what I have? A desk that's big enough," Sara
had said and which I could see now as we sat opposite
the bathtub in the kitchen of her newplace
where we talked away a good part of the afternoon re-
considering sex into a status satellite to dialog/work
hanging out/sport while another a third poet currently
doing what she does in Seattle came into the room
by cassette

"I have loved you assiduously" Trazana Beverley's voice
advertising *for colored girls* cracks me up on my

way to the airport/*assiduously* on the FM (yeah Zaki!) on
my way to pick up Louise wiped out by Cambridge where
she proved the muse is female on
paper
and
all this stuff going on and my lover wants to know
am I a feminist or what and what does the question
mean I mean
or *what?*

A Poem about Intelligence for My Brothers and Sisters

A few years back and they told me Black
means a hole where other folks
got brain/it was like the cells in the heads
of Black children was out to every hour on the hour naps
Scientists called the phenomenon the Notorious
Jensen Lapse, remember?
Anyway I was thinking
about how to devise
a test for the wise
like a Stanford-Binet
for the C.I.A.
you know?
Take Einstein
being the most the unquestionable the outstanding
the maximal mind of the century
right?
And I'm struggling against this lapse leftover
from my Black childhood to fathom why
anybody should say so:
$E=mc$ squared?
I try that on this old lady live on my block:
She sweeping away Saturday night from the stoop
and mad as can be because some absolute
jackass have left a kingsize mattress where
she have to sweep around it stains and all she
don't want to know nothing about in the first place
"Mrs. Johnson!" I say, leaning on the gate
between us: "What you think about somebody come up
with an E equals M C 2?"
"How you doin," she answer me, sideways, like she don't
want to let on she know I ain'

combed my hair yet and here it is
Sunday morning but still I have the nerve
to be bothering serious work with these crazy
questions about
"*E* equals what you say again, dear?"
Then I tell her, "Well
also this same guy? I think
he was undisputed Father of the Atom Bomb!"
"That right." She mumbles or grumbles, not too politely
"And dint remember to wear socks when he put on
his shoes!" I add on (getting desperate)
at which point Mrs. Johnson take herself and her broom
a very big step down the stoop away from me
"And never did nothing for nobody in particular
lessen it was a committee
and
used to say, 'What time is it?'
and
you'd say, 'Six o'clock.'
and
he'd say, 'Day or night?'
and
and he never made nobody a cup a tea
in his whole brilliant life!
and
[my voice rises slightly]
and
he dint never boogie neither: never!"

"Well," say Mrs. Johnson, "Well, honey,
I do guess
that's genius for you."

"Haruko:"

"Haruko:
Oh! It's like <u>stringbean</u> in French?"

"No:
It's like <u>hurricane</u>
in English!"

Poem on the Death of Princess Diana

At least she was riding
beside
somebody going somewhere
fast
about love

Winter Honey

Sugar come
and sugar go
Sugar dumb
but sugar know
ain' nothin' run me for my money
nothin' sweet like winter honey

Sugar high
and sugarlow
Sugar pie
and sugar dough
Then sugar throw
a sugar fit
And sugar find
a sugar tit
But never mind
what sugar find
ain' nothin' run me for my money
nothin' sweet like winter honey

Sugar come
and please don' go
Sugar dumb
but oh-my: Oh!
Ain' nothin' run me for my money
nothin' sweet like winter honey

On a New Year's Eve

Infinity doesn't interest me

not altogether
anymore

I crawl and kneel and grub about
I beg and listen for

what can go away

                    (as easily as love)
or perish
like the children
running
hard on oneway streets/infinity
doesn't interest me

not anymore

not even
repetition your/my/eye-
lid or the colorings of sunrise
or all the sky excitement
added up

is not enough

to satisfy this lusting adulation that I feel
for
your brown arm before it
moves

MOVES
CHANGES UP

the temporary sacred
tales ago
first bikeride round the house
when you first saw a squat
opossum
carry babies on her back
opossum up
in the persimmon tree
you reeling toward
that natural
first
absurdity
with so much wonder still
it shakes your voice

                    the temporary is the sacred
                    takes me out

and even the stars and even the snow and even
the rain
do not amount to much
unless these things submit to some disturbance
some derangement such
as when I yield myself/belonging
to your unmistaken
body

and let the powerful lock up the canyon/mountain
peaks the
hidden rivers/waterfalls the
deepdown minerals/the coalfields/goldfields/

diamond mines close by the whoring ore
hot
at the center of the earth

spinning fast as numbers
I cannot imagine

let the world blot
obliterate remove so-
called
magnificence
so-called
almighty/fathomless and everlasting/
treasures/
wealth
(whatever that may be)
it is this time
that matters

it is this history
I care about

the one we make together
awkward
inconsistent
as a lame cat on the loose
or quick as kids freed by the bell
or else as strictly
once
as only life must mean
a once upon a time

I have rejected propaganda teaching me
about the beautiful
the truly rare

(supposedly
the soft push of the ocean at the hushpoint of the shore
supposedly
the soft push of the ocean at the hushpoint of the shore
is beautiful
for instance)
but
the truly rare can stay out there

I have rejected that
abstraction that enormity
unless I see a dog walk on the beach/
a bird seize sandflies
or yourself
approach me
laughing out a sound to spoil
the pretty picture
make an uncontrolled
heartbeating memory
instead

I read the papers preaching on
that oil and oxygen
that redwoods and the evergreens
that trees the waters and the atmosphere
compile a final listing of the world in
short supply

but all alive and all the lives
persist perpetual
in jeopardy
persist
as scarce as every one of us
as difficult to find

or keep
as irreplaceable
as frail
as every one of us

and
as I watch your arm/your
brown arm
just
before it moves

I know

all things are dear
that disappear

*all things are dear
that disappear*

[·]

1977: Poem for Mrs. Fannie Lou Hamer

You used to say, "June?
Honey when you come down here you
supposed to stay with me. Where
else?"
Meanin home
against the beer the shotguns and the
point of view of whitemen don'
never see Black anybodies without
some violent itch start up.
                            The ones who
said, "No Nigga's Votin in This Town . . .
lessen it be feet first to the booth"
Then jailed you
beat you brutal
bloody/battered/beat
you blue beyond the feeling
of the terrible

And failed to stop you.
Only God could but He
wouldn't stop
you
fortress from self-
pity

Humble as a woman anywhere
I remember finding you inside the laundromat
in Ruleville
          lion spine relaxed/hell
          what's the point to courage
          when you washin clothes?

But that took courage

> just to sit there/target
> to the killers lookin
> for your singin face
> perspirey through the rinse
> and spin

and later
you stood mighty in the door on James Street
loud callin:

> "BULLETS OR NO BULLETS!
> THE FOOD IS COOKED
> AN' GETTIN COLD!"

We ate
A family tremulous but fortified
by turnips/okra/handpicked
like the lilies

filled to the very living
full

one solid gospel
> *(sanctified)*

one gospel
> *(peace)*

one full Black lily
luminescent
in a homemade field

of love

In the Times of My Heart

In the times of my heart
the children tell the clock
a hallelujah
        listen people
        listen

The Reception

Doretha wore the short blue lace last night
and William watched her drinking so she fight
with him in flying collar slim-jim orange
tie and alligator belt below the navel pants uptight

"I flirt. You hear me? Yes I flirt.
Been on my pretty knees all week
to clean the rich white downtown dirt
the greedy garbage money reek.

I flirt. Damned right. You look at me."
But William watched her carefully
his mustache shaky she could see
him jealous, "which is how he always be

at parties." Clementine and Wilhelmina
looked at trouble in the light blue lace
and held to George while Roosevelt Senior
circled by the yella high and bitterly light blue face

he liked because she worked
the crowded room like clay like molding men
from dust to muscle jerked
and arms and shoulders moving when

she moved. The Lord Almighty Seagrams bless
Doretha in her short blue dress
and Roosevelt waiting for his chance:
a true gut-funky blues to make her really dance.

Poem for Mark

England, I thought, will look like Africa
or India with elephants and pale men
pushing things about
rifle and gloves
handlebar mustache and tea
pith helmets
riding crop
The Holy Bible
and a rolled up map of plunder
possibilities

But schoolboys with schoolbags
little enough for sweets
wore Wellingtons into the manicured
mud
and Cockney manners
("I say
we've been waiting 45 minutes
for this bus, we 'ave! It's
a regular disgrace,
it 'tis!"
"Yes, love: I'm sorry! But
step up/move along,
now! I'm doing the best I can!
You can
write a letter if you please!")
quite outclassed the Queen's

And time felt like a flag
right side up and flying
high while mousse-spike haircuts
denim jackets strolled around

and Afro-Caribbean/Afro-Celtic men
and women comfortable in full
length Rasta dreads
invited me to dinner
or presented me with poetry

And we
sat opposite but close
debating Nicaragua
or the civil liberties of countries
under siege
and you said
"Rubbish!" to the notion of a national
identity
and if I answered,
"In my country—"
You would interrupt me, saying,
"You're not serious!"
but then I thought I was
about "my country"
meaning where I'd come from
recently
and after only transatlantic static for a single
phone call
up against my loathing to disrupt and travel
to the silly land of Philip and Diana
never having hoped for anyone (a bebop-
antelope) like you
so quietly impertinent and teasing
it was 4 a.m. the first time
when we stopped the conversation
And long before my face lay nestling on the hotel
pillows/well
I knew

whoever the hell "my people"
are
I knew that one of them
is you

Sunflower Sonnet Number Two

Supposing we could just go on and on as two
voracious in the days apart as well as when
we side by side (the many ways we do
that) well! I would consider then
perfection possible, or else worthwhile
to think about. Which is to say
I guess the costs of long term tend to pile
up, block and complicate, erase away
the accidental, temporary, near
thing/pulsebeat promises one makes
because the chance, the easy new, is there
in front of you. But still, perfection takes
some sacrifice of falling stars for rare.
And there are stars, but none of you, to spare.

After All Is Said and Done

Maybe you thought I would forget
about the sunrise
how the moon stayed in the morning
time a lower lip
your partly open partly spoken
mouth

Maybe you thought I would exaggerate
the fire of the stars
the fire of the wet wood burning by
the waterside
the fire of the fuck the sudden move
you made me make
to meet you
(fire)

BABY
I do not exaggerate and
if
I could
I would.

Shakespeare's 116th Sonnet in Black English Translation

Don't let me mess up partner happiness
because the trouble
start
An' I ain' got the heart
to deal!
That won't be real
(about love)
if I
(push come to shove)
just punk

Not hardly! Hey:
Love do not cooperate
with cop-out
provocations: No!

Storm come. Storm go
away
but love stay
steady
(if you ready or
you not!)
True love stay
steady
True love stay
hot!

Exercise in Quits

November 15, 1969

1

               moratorium means well what
you think it means you
dense? Stop it means stop.

We move and we march sing songs
move march sing songs move march move

It/stop means stop.

            hey mister man

how long you been fixing to kill somebody?
Waste of time
            the preparation training

you was born a bullet.

2

we be wondering what they gone do
all them others left and right
what they have in mind

about us
and who by the way is "us"

listen you got a match you got the light
you got two eyes two hands
why you taking pictures of the people
what you sposed to be you

got to photograph the people?

you afraid you will (otherwise) forget
what people look like?

man
or however you been paying dues

we look like you

                on second thought
there is a clear resemblance to the dead
among the living so

go ahead go on
and take my picture

quick

"Why I became a pacifist"

Why I became a pacifist
and then
How I became a warrior again:

Because nothing I could do or say
turned out okay
I figured I should just sit
still and chill
except to maybe mumble
"Baby, Baby:
Stop!"
AND
Because turning that other cheek
      holding my tongue
      refusing to retaliate when the deal
      got ugly
And because not throwing whoever calls me *bitch*
      out the goddamn window
And because swallowing my pride
      saying I'm sorry when whoever don't like
      one single thing
      about me and don't never take a break from
      counting up the 65,899 ways I talk wrong
      I act wrong
And because sitting on my fist
      neglecting to enumerate every incoherent
      rigid/raggedy-ass/disrespectful/killer cold
      and self-infatuated crime against love
      committed by some loudmouth don't know
      nothing about it takes 2 to fuck and
      it takes 2 to fuck things up

And because making apologies that nobody give a shit about

and because failing to sing my song

finally
finally

   got on my absolute last nerve

I pick up my sword
I lift up my shield
And I stay ready for war
Because now I live ready for a whole lot more

than that

Poem for Siddhārtha Gautama of the Shākyas: The Original Buddha

You say, "Close your eye to the butterfly!"
I say, "Don't blink!"

Calling on All Silent Minorities

HEY

C'MON
COME OUT

WHEREVER YOU ARE

WE NEED TO HAVE THIS MEETING
AT THIS TREE

AIN' EVEN BEEN
PLANTED
YET

Poem Number Two on Bell's Theorem, or
The New Physicality of Long Distance Love

There is no chance that we will fall apart
There is no chance
There are no parts.

Memoranda toward the Spring of Seventy-Nine

The Shah of Iran was overthrown
by only several million mostly un-
armed/inside agitators.

~

The Daily News reports that one American
among the first to be evacuated, Patsy
Farness of Seattle, said she somehow en-
joyed the whole thing. Coming off the plane
with two Persian cats and a poodle, she said:
"It was a lovely experience. I didn't want
to leave."

~

The instruction booklet for cooking with a
Chinese wok declares as follows: "With use
your wok will acquire the blackened look of
distinction."

~

Martin Luther King, Jr., is still dead.
The sponsor for the memorial program on
his birthday is The National Boat Show
at the Coliseum running January 13th through
the 21st and open to the public.

~

If only I could stay awake until 3
then
on Channel Eleven

I could watch Part One of Adolf Hitler
but
then I'd be too tired to get up by 8
to watch Kaptain Kangaroo and Woody Woodpecker
on Channels 2 and 5.

~

The Shah of Iran was overthrown
by only several million mostly un-
armed/inside agitators.

~

There must be something else on television.

~

Martin Luther King, Jr., is still dead.

~

Dear Abby,

The idea is two dozen red roses
but
there isn't any form around the house.
Please advise.

Scenario Revision #1

Or
suppose that gorgeous
wings spread
speckled
hawk
begins to glide
above my body lying
down
like dead meat
maybe start to rot
a little bit
not moving
see just flat
just limp
but hot
not moving
see
him circle closer
closing closer
for the kill
until
he makes that dive
to savage
me
and inches
from the blood flood lusty
beak
I roll away
I speak
I laugh out loud

Not yet
big bird of prey
not yet

For Alice Walker (a summertime tanka)

Redwood grove and war
You and me talking Congo
gender grief and ash

I say, "God! It's all so huge"
You say, "These sweet trees: This tree"

Free Flight

Nothing fills me up at night
I fall asleep for one or two hours then
up again my gut
alarms
I must arise
and wandering into the refrigerator
think about evaporated milk homemade vanilla ice cream
cherry pie hot from the oven with Something Like Vermont
Cheddar Cheese disintegrating luscious
on the top while
mildly
I devour almonds and raisins mixed to mathematical
criteria or celery or my very own sweet and sour snack
composed of brie peanut butter honey and
a minuscule slice of party size salami
on a single whole wheat cracker *no salt added*
or I read César Vallejo/Gabriela Mistral/last year's
complete anthology or
I might begin another list of things to do
that starts with toilet paper and
I notice that I never jot down fresh
strawberry shortcake: never
even though fresh strawberry shortcake shoots down
raisins and almonds 6 to nothing
effortlessly
effortlessly
is this poem on my list?
light bulbs lemons envelopes ballpoint refill
post office and zucchini
oranges no
it's not

I guess that means I just forgot
walking my dog around the block leads
to a space in my mind where
during the newspaper strike questions
sizzle through suddenly like
Is there an earthquake down in Ecuador?
Did a T.W.A. supersaver flight to San Francisco
land in Philadelphia instead
or
whatever happened to human rights
in Washington D.C.? Or what about downward destabilization
of the consumer price index
and I was in this school P.S. Tum-Ta-Tum and time came
for me to leave but
No! I couldn't leave: The Rule was anybody leaving
the premises without having taught somebody something
valuable would be henceforth proscribed from the
premises would be forever null and void/dull and
vilified well
I had stood in front of 40 to 50 students running my
mouth and I had been generous with deceitful smiles/soft-
spoken and pseudo-gentle wiles if and when forced
into discourse amongst such adults as constitutes
the regular treacheries of On The Job Behavior
ON THE JOB BEHAVIOR
is this poem on that list
polish shoes file nails coordinate tops and bottoms
lipstick control no
screaming I'm bored because
this is whoring away the hours of god's creation
pay attention to your eyes your hands the twilight
sky in the institutional big windows
no

I did not presume I was not so bold as to put this
poem on that list
then at the end of the class this boy gives me Mahler's 9th
symphony the double album listen
to it let it seep into you he
says transcendental love
he says
I think naw
I been angry all day long/nobody did the assignment
I am not prepared
I am not prepared for so much grace
the catapulting music of surprise that makes me
hideaway my face
nothing fills me up at night
yesterday the houseguest left a brown
towel in the bathroom for tonight
I set out a blue one and
an off-white washcloth seriously
I don't need no houseguest
I don't need no towels/lovers
I just need a dog

Maybe I'm kidding

Maybe I need a woman
a woman be so well you know so wifelike
so more or less motherly so listening so much
the universal skin you love to touch and who the
closer she gets to you the better she looks to me/somebody
say yes and make me laugh and tell me she know she
been there she spit bullets at my enemies she say you
need to sail around Alaska fuck it all try this new
cerebral tea and take a long bath

Maybe I need a man
a man be so well you know so manly so lifelike
so more or less virile so sure so much the deep
voice of opinion and the shoulders like a window
seat and cheeks so closely shaven by a twin-edged
razor blade no oily hair and no dandruff besides/
somebody say yes and make
me laugh and tell me he know he been there he spit
bullets at my enemies he say you need to sail around
Alaska fuck it all and take a long bath

lah-ti-dah and lah-ti-dum
what's this socialized obsession with the bathtub

Maybe I just need to love myself myself
(anyhow I'm more familiar with the subject)
Maybe when my cousin tells me you remind me
of a woman past her prime maybe I need
to hustle my cousin into a hammerlock
position make her cry out uncle and
I'm sorry
Maybe when I feel this horrible
inclination to kiss folks I despise
because the party's like that
an occasion to be kissing people
you despise maybe I should tell them kindly
kiss my

Maybe when I wake up in the middle of the night
I should go downstairs
dump the refrigerator contents on the floor
and stand there in the middle of the spilled milk
and the wasted butter spread beneath my dirty feet
writing poems

writing poems
maybe I just need to love myself myself and
anyway
I'm working on it

Not Looking

Not looking now and then I find you here
not knowing where you are.
Talk to me. Tell me the things I see
fill the table between us or surround
the precipice nobody dares to forget.
Talking takes time takes everything
sooner than I can forget the precipice
and speak to your being there
where I hear you move no nearer
than you were standing on my hands
covered my eyes dreaming about music.

On the Spirit of Mildred Jordan

After sickness and a begging
from her bed
my mother dressed herself
gray lace-up oxfords
stockings baggy on her shrunken legs
an orange topper
rhinestone buttons
and a powder blue straw
hat with plastic
flowers

Then
she took the street
in short steps toward the corner

chewing gum
no less

she let the family laugh
again

she wasn't foxy
she was strong

Meta-Rhetoric

Homophobia
racism
self-definition
revolutionary struggle

the subject tonight for
public discussion is
our love

we sit apart
apparently at opposite ends of a line
and I feel the distance
between my eyes
between my legs
a dry
dust topography of our separation

In the meantime people
dispute the probabilities
of union

They reminisce about the chasmic histories
no ideology yet dares to surmount

I disagree with you
You disagree with me
The problem seems to be a matter of scale

Can you give me the statistical dimensions
of your mouth on my mouth
your breasts resting on my own?

I believe the agenda involves
several inches (at least)
of coincidence and endless recovery

My hope is that our lives will declare
this meeting
open

Poem for South African Women

*Commemoration of the 40,000 women and
children who, August 9, 1956, presented
themselves in bodily protest against the
"dompas" in the capital of apartheid. Presented
at the United Nations, August 9, 1978.*

Our own shadows disappear as the feet of thousands
by the tens of thousands pound the fallow land
into new dust that
rising like a marvelous pollen will be
fertile
even as the first woman whispering
imagination to the trees around her made
for righteous fruit
from such deliberate defense of life
as no other still
will claim inferior to any other safety
in the world

The whispers too they
intimate to the inmost ear of every spirit
now aroused they
carousing in ferocious affirmation
of all peaceable and loving amplitude
sound a certainly unbounded heat
from a baptismal smoke where yes
there will be fire

And the babies cease alarm as mothers
raising arms
and heart high as the stars so far unseen
nevertheless hurl into the universe

a moving force
irreversible as light years
traveling to the open
eye

And who will join this standing up
and the ones who stood without sweet company
will sing and sing
back into the mountains and
if necessary
even under the sea

we are the ones we have been waiting for

July 4, 1984: For Buck

April 7, 1978–June 16, 1984

You would shrink back/jump up
cock ears/shake head
tonight
at this bloody idea of a birthday
represented by smackajack explosions
of percussive lunacy and downright
(blowawayavillage) boom boom
ratatat-tat-zap

Otherwise any threat would make you stand
quivering perfect as a story
no amount of repetition could hope to ruin
perfect as the kangaroo boogie you concocted
with a towel in your jaws and your tail
tucked under and your paws
speeding around the ecstatic circle
of your refutation of the rain
outdoors

And mostly you would lunge electrical
and verge into the night
ears practically on flat alert
nostrils on the agitated sniff
(for falling rawhide meteors) and laugh
at compliments galore and then
teach me to love you
by hand
teach me to love you
by heart

as I do now

Something like a Sonnet for Phillis Miracle Wheatley

Girl from the realm of birds florid and fleet
flying full feather in far or near weather
Who fell to a dollar lust coffled like meat
Captured by avarice and hate spit together
Trembling asthmatic alone on the slave block
built by a savagery traveling by carriage
viewed like a species of flaw in the livestock
A child without safety of mother or marriage

Chosen by whimsy but born to surprise
They taught you to read but you learned how to write
Begging the universe into your eyes:
They dressed you in light but you dreamed with the night.
From Africa singing of justice and grace,
Your early verse sweetens the fame of our Race.

Poem about Heartbreak That Go On and On

bad love last like a big
ugly lizard crawl around the house
forever
never die
and never change itself

into a butterfly

Poem for a Young Poet

Dedicated to Erwin Cho-Woods
May 27, 1997

Most people search all
of their lives
for someplace to belong to
as you said
but I look instead
into the eyes of anyone
who talks to me

I search for a face
to believe and belong to
a loosening mask
with a voice
ears
and a consciousness
breathing through
a nose
I can see

Day to day
it's the only way
I like to travel
noticing the colors of a cheek
the curvature of brow
and the public declarations
of two lips

Okay!
I did not say male
or female

I did not say Serbian
or Tutsi
I said
what tilts my head
into the opposite of fear
or dread
is anyone
who talks to me

A face
to claim or question
my next step away
or else towards

fifteen anemones
dilated well beyond apologies
for such an open centerpiece
that soft
forever begs for bees

one morning
and the birdsong and the dew-
struck honeysuckle blending
invitations to dislodge
my fingers tangling with my sunlit
lover's hair

A face
to spur or interdict
my mesmerized approach
or else
my agonized reproach

to strangulations of the soul
that bring a mother

to disown
her children
leaving them alone to feed
on bone and dust

A face
despite a corpse
invasion of the cradle
where I rock my love
alive

A face
despite numb fashions
of an internet connection between nobody
and no one

A face
against the narcoleptic/antiseptic
chalk streaks
in the sky
that lie
and posit credit cards
and starched de facto exposés
as copacetic evidence
that you and I
need no defense
against latrine
and bully bullet-proof decisions
launched by limousines
dividing up the big screen
into gold points
cold above the valley
of the shadow of unpardonable
tiny

tiny
tiny
this breathing and that breath
and then
that and that
that death

I search a face
a loosening mask
with voice
ears
and a consciousness
breathing through
a nose
that I can see

I search a face
for obstacles to genocide
I search beyond the dead
and
driven by imperfect visions
of the living
yes and no
I come and go
back to the eyes
of anyone
who talks to me

Democracy Poem #1

Tell them that I stood
in line
and I waited
and I waited
like everybody
else

But I never got
called
And I keep that scrap
of paper
in my pocket

just in case

[·]

Poem from Taped Testimony in the Tradition of Bernhard Goetz

1

This was not I repeat this was not a racial incident.

2

I was sitting down and it happened to me
before that I was sitting down or I was standing
up and I was by myself because of course
a lot of the time I am by myself because
I am not married or famous or super-im-
portant enough to have shadows or body-
guards so I was alone as it happens when
I was sitting down or let me retract that
I wasn't with anybody else regardless
who else was there
and I know I am not blind I could see
other people around me but the point
is that I wasn't with them I wasn't
with anybody else and like I said
it happened before two three
times it had happened that I was
sitting down or I was standing up
when one of them or one time it was
more than one I think it was two
of them anyway they just jumped
me I mean they jumped on me like
I was chump change and I know
I am not blind I could see they were
laughing at me they thought it was
funny to make me feel humiliated or I don't

know ugly or weak or really too small
to fight back so they were just laughing
at me in a way I mean you didn't
necessarily see some kind of a smile
or hear them laughing but I could feel
it like I could feel I could always
feel this shiver thing this fear take
me over when I would have to come into a room
full of them and I would be by myself
and they would just look at you know what
I mean you can't know what I mean
you're not Black

3

How would you know
how that feels when mostly you move through
outnumbered and you are the one doesn't
fit in doesn't look right doesn't read
right because you're not white
but you live
in this place in this city where
again and again
there you are inside but outside or off
and you're different and I would never know when
it would happen again that the talking
would stop or the talking would start
or somebody would say something
stupid or nasty to me like nigga
or honey or bitch or not say
anything at all like the drugstore on Sunday
and I was standing in line but the girl
behind the counter couldn't get it
together to say, "Yes. Can I help

you?" or anything at all she was counting
on silence to make me
disappear or beg or I don't know
what and okay I'm visiting New Hampshire
but also
I live here I mean in this country
I live here and you should have seen
the look of her eyes they were shining
I know I am not blind and she wanted
to make believe me this irreducible this me
into a no-count what you gone do about
it/zip

4

So one of them a policeman a long
time ago but I remember it he kicked
in the teeth of Jeffrey Underwood who
lived on my block and who had been the best
looking boy in the neighborhood and he was tall
and skinny even and kind of shy and he/
Jeffrey went up on the roof with fire
crackers I mean it was the roof of the house
of a family that knew him and they knew
Jeffrey's parents too and
my cousin told me the next morning how
this policeman asked Jeffrey to come
down so Jeffrey left the roof and came
down to the street where we lived and
then the policeman beat Jeffrey
unconscious and he/the
policeman who was one of them he kicked
Jeffrey's teeth out and I never wanted to see
Jeffrey anymore but I kept seeing

these policemen and I remember how
my cousin who was older than I was I remember how
she whispered to me, "That's what they
do to you"

5

and the stinging of my face when some of
them my mother told me they were
Irish and when some of them shot at me
with zip guns and howled out "li'l nigga"
I was eight years old by myself walking
with my book bag to a public school
and I remember my mother
asking me to kneel down beside her to pray
for the Irish

6

So much later and of course this is not something
I keep on the front burner but then again
it's nothing you want to forget because
enough is enough and it has happened before
and it happens so often but when you turn around
for help or the punishment of these people
where can you go I mean I was raped six
years ago by one of them who was good he told me
with a rifle and he raped me and his
brother was the judge in town and so forth all
of them have brothers all over town there
are so many of them everywhere you go so
either you become the routine
setup
or you have to figure out
some self-defense

7

I was sitting down and it had happened
before that I was sitting down and I was
by myself because not one of them was
with me not one of them was cognizant
(to use a better word) of me where I
was sitting down and they filled up
the room around me and one of them
sat down to my left and another one
of them sat down beside my right fist
on the table (next to the silverware) and
I was sitting there quiet and mild-
mannered which is how I am you can
ask my neighbors you can read about
it in the papers everyday the papers
tell you I am quiet and mild-mannered which is
how I sat there at this table in a room
full of them and then the one to the right
of my right fist she started up about this South
African novel she was reading and she said to the one
to my left by which I mean she ignored me in the middle
and it felt like I was
not there but I was I was sitting
in my chair at the table where
she the one to my right said to the one
to my left she said, "And the writer
expects the reader to be sympathetic
to that character!" And then the
one to my left said to the one to my
right she said, "Exactly! And it's
so cheap. It's so disgusting. She (the
writer) makes her (the character)

marry not one but two Black revolutionaries!" And
        something snapped
inside me I could see across the table
more of them just sitting there eyes
shining
and I know I am not blind
I could see them laughing at me and I went
cold because in a situation like that
you have to be cold a cold
killer or they will ridicule you
right there at the dining table and
I wanted to murder
I wanted them to hurt and bleed I wanted
them to leave me alone
and so I became cold I became a cold
killer and I took out my gun and
I shot the one to my right and then
I shot the one to my left and then I looked
across the table and I thought, "They
look all right," and so I shot them too
and it was self-defense I wanted
them to stop playing with me
I wanted them to know it's not cheap
or disgusting to love a Black
revolutionary and
as a matter of fact
I wanted them to know you'd
better love a Black revolutionary before she
gets the idea

that you don't

On Time Tanka

I refuse to choose
between lynch rope and gang rape
the blues is the blues!
my skin and my sex: Deep dues
I have no wish to escape

I refuse to lose
the flame of my single space
this safety I choose
between your fist and my face
between my gender and race

All black and blue news
withers the heart of my hand
and leads to abuse
no one needs to understand:
suicide wipes out the clues

Big-Time-Juicy-Fruit!
Celebrity-Rich-Hero
Rollin out the Rolls!
Proud cheatin on your (Black) wife
Loud beatin on your (white) wife

Real slime open mouth
police officer-true-creep
evil-and-uncouth
fixin to burn black people
killin the song of our sleep

Neither one of you
gets any play in my day

I know what you do
your money your guns your say
so against my pepper spray

Okay! laugh away!
I hear you and I accuse
you both: I refuse
to choose: All black and blue news
means that I hurt and I lose.

In Defense of Christianity: Sermon from the Fount

dedicated to John Ashcroft, Inc.

"And seeing the multitudes
he closed up his laptop
computer
and because the multitudes let him begin
to imagine a global market
big
bigger than anybody's kingdom
of heaven
he cleared his throat
he gulped a pretty cool
gulp of natural
spring water
and speaking into the omni-
directional microphone
at last
he spoke out loud
he spoke to the multitudes
saying
Blessed are the rich: For theirs will be the wealth of the world!

Woe to the poor! for they will find it difficult
to eat the eye of a camel
with or without a needle!

Blessed are the blithe and the oblivious
for they shall require no comfort!

Blessed are the proud and the mighty: For they shall conquer
the earth and subdivide
and subjugate the peoples who abide
therein!

Blessed are they who inherit inheritance and who
do away with inheritance taxation so that they
like the lilies of the field
they and their children and their children's children
shall prosper without toil and flourish without sweat!

Blessed are they which do preach and pursue
supremacy
for they shall rule supreme and cleanse our tribes
of all impurities
even as an infinitesimal mustard seed shall become
a huge tree where birds of the air
find refuge
even so
even the seeds of supremacy shall spread
and shelter
everyone whosoever
believes!

If any man shall smite thee on thy right
cheek
amputate his arms and turn also thy sword
against his family and his village!

If any man or nation-state shall injure
or otherwise diminish indispensable self-esteem
you shall decapitate that man
you shall obliterate that nation-state
even unto the third and following
generations!

Blessed are they who make conspicuous
and compulsory
public display of piety

and who advertise such obvious
parade
as virtue!

Blessed are they who worship the magic
of money and the mythology of gold and who
prostrate themselves to profit-making
and who despise and ostracize the unprofitable
elements among us!

For, verily, this is my particular commandment unto you:

Do unto others as reliable market indicators
shall clearly counsel, or proscribe!

But above and beyond all else, Judge that ye be not judged!
Judge that ye be not judged!

And, so saying,
And having so said,
he left the multitudes behind

as he stepped aboard
a gleaming
luxury yacht
waiting for him and his
disciples only
on the Sea of Galilee
he just sailed
away"

Poem on Sexual Hysteria and Sexual Hypocrisy

DeLiza
want more information
about inappropriate or appropriate
relations

She scowl

She prowl through big book
don' say diddly-
squat
about "that
woman"
or this man
seem like he can'
never remember nobody's
name

DeLiza
shake she dread lock head

How come
or who come
or whassup
or who's down

and why
she have to hear
about 2 overgrown
libidinous dogs
doing or not doing
whatever

dogs
do

DeLiza
take that back
      dogs do not forget
      dogs do not feel regret
      dogs do not flirt
      in or with
      a miniskirt
      dogs do not seek and hide
      no kinda pleasure
      dogs do not treasure
      the evidence of some
      old bone
      dogs tell
      nosey people
            "Go to hell"
      dogs do not wait
      until everything's too late
      dogs moving right along
      where dogs belong
      with other dogs
      dogs

do not carry on
appropriate
or inappropriate
relationships

so

DeLiza clear about dogs
but

she confounded by two overgrown
libidinous homo saps
who
allow a public prostitution who
permit
a public prosecution
of they private jive
and jam

because
truly she do not give a damn
because
DeLiza know
DeLiza ain' about to take
no stupid Starr-Tripp

ever!

Manifesto of the Rubber Gloves

So I'm wearing brand new loud blue
Rubber gloves
because
I'm serious about I don't wanna die
from
mainstream contamination
mainstream
poison water poisonous
like
statistical majorities
that represent
poison waters poisonous
like
neo-nazi perspectives
that reflect
the mainstream
poison waters
like
scapegoat policies
that distill
the mainstream
poison waters poisonous
like
the Congress and the Governor and the President
and the Supremely Clarence Retrograde Thomas
Court
of Separated and Unequal
and Proud about That
Last Resort

I'm wearing brand new loud blue
Rubber gloves
because
I'm serious about I don't wanna die
from
mainstream contamination
mainstream
poison waters poisonous
like the F.B.I. and the A.T.F.
and the I.N.S. and Secret Service
Security Guards
with or without a cut on anybody's finger
and a pointless
overblown Armed Force
afraid to fight
unless
it gets a not-a-single-cut-on-a-single-one-
of-your-fingers guarantee
backed by
a would-be
hero's welcome
just for hiding the hell
out of trouble
when the point
might very well
be
"The trouble"
The 600,000 human beings already dead
anyway
in Bosnia

I'm wearing brand new loud blue
Rubber gloves
because I'm serious about I don't wanna die

from
mainstream contamination
poison waters poisonous
like
a serial killer
start anyplace
(next door!)
and slash and dismember
and move on
and on and kill more and more
a serial killer
absolutely
mainstream
tall and good
(looking)
nicely dressed
a dedicated
fast-traveling
serial killer
straight from the heart land oozing
mainstream
poison waters
a Republican (or Democrat)
a soft spoken young man
a believer in Christ Jesus
a serial killer
like
The Pilgrims
like
the early
serial killer
pioneers
beginning
with anybody indigenous

and then *x y z*
and then *a b c*
and always
beating up
and always
hunting down
the poor
and
the niggers
and
the kikes
and
the wetbacks
and
the chinks
and
the faggots
and
the dykes

I'm serious about I don't wanna die
from
mainstream
poison waters poisonous
at flood-tide heights
and depths
of programmatic/legislative/circular
self-righteous/white
black/Baptist/Vatican
or secular
or in-between
or accidental/multi-ethnic

consecration
to my death!

I'm wearing brand new loud blue
Rubber gloves
because
I'm serious about I don't wanna die
from
mainstream contamination
mainstream
poison waters poisonous
and swollen
all around me
and
as far as I can see

I'm serious
because
I don't wanna die
I don't wanna die
I don't wanna die

Kissing God Goodbye

Poem in the face of Operation Rescue
Dedicated to Jennie Portnoff

You mean to tell me on the 12th day or the 13th
that the Lord
which is to say some wiseass
got more muscle than he
reasonably
can control or figure out/some
accidental hard disk
thunderbolt/some
big mouth
woman-hating/super
heterosexist heterosexual
kind of a guy guy
he decided who could live and who would die?

And after he did what?
created alleyways of death
and acid rain
and infant mortality rates
and sons of the gun
and something called the kitchenette
and trailer trucks to kill and carry
beautiful trees out of their natural
habitat/Oh! Not that guy?

Was it that other guy
who invented a snake
an apple and a really
retarded scenario so that
down to this very day

it is not a lot of fun
to give birth to a son of a gun?
And wasn't no woman in the picture
of the Lord?
He done the whole thing by himself?
The oceans and the skies
and the fish that swim and the bird
that flies?

You sure he didn't have some serious problems
of perspective
for example
coming up with mountains/valleys/rivers/rainbows
and no companionship/no coach/no
midwife/boyfriend/girlfriend/
no help whatsoever for a swollen
overactive
brain
unable to spell
sex

You mean to tell me that the planet
is the brainchild
of a single
      male
      head of household?

And everything he said and done
the floods/famines/plagues
and pestilence
the invention of the slave and the invention of the gun
the worship of war (especially whichever war
he won)
And after everything he thought about and made 2 million

megapronouncements about
(Like)
"Give not your strength to women"
and
"You shall not lie with a male as with a woman"
and
"An outsider shall not eat of a holy thing"
and
"If a woman conceives and bears a male child
then she shall be unclean
seven days . . . But if she bears
a female child, then she shall be unclean
2 weeks . . ."
and
"The leper who has the disease
shall wear torn clothes and let the hair
of his head hang loose
and he shall cover his upper lip
and cry, 'Unclean,
unclean!'"
and
"Behold, I have 2 daughters
who have not known a man,
let me bring them out to you, and do
to them as you please"
and
"I will greatly multiply your pain
in childbearing:
in pain shall you bring forth children"
and
"Take your son, your only son Isaac,
whom you love,
and go to the land of Moriah, and offer
him there as a burnt offering"

and in the middle of this lunatic lottery
there was Ruth saying to Naomi:
"Entreat me not
to leave you or to return
from following you; for where you go
I will go
and where you lodge I will lodge, your people
shall be my people
And your God my God;
where you die I will die,
and there I will be buried. May the Lord do so to me
and more also
if even death parts me from you."
and
David wailing aloud at the death of Jonathan who loved him
"more than his own soul" and David
inconsolable in lamentation
saying
". . . very pleasant have you been to me;
your love to me was wonderful,
passing the love of women"
and
"If I give away all I have, and if I deliver
my body to be burned,
but have not love,
I gain nothing . . ."
and this chaos/this chaos
exploded tyrannical in scattershot scripture
(Like)
". . . those who belong in Christ
Jesus have crucified the flesh
with its passions and desire"
and
"Cast out the slave and her son"

and
"If in spite of this you will not hearken
to me, then . . .
You shall eat the flesh of your sons,
you shall eat the flesh
of your daughters. And I will
destroy your high places . . . I will
lay your cities waste . . . I will
devastate your land . . . And
as for those of you that are left,
I will send faintness
into their hearts in the lands of their enemies
the sound of a driven leaf
shall put them to flight . . ."
etcetera etcetera
That guy?
That guy?
the ruler of all earth
and heaven too
The maker of all laws
and all taboo
The absolute supremacist
of power
the origin of the destiny
of molecules and Mars
The father and the son
the king and the prince
The prophet and the prophecy
The singer and the song
The man from whom
in whom
of whom
by whom
comes everything

without the womb
without that unclean
feminine
connection/
that guy?

The emperor of poverty
The czar of suffering
The wizard of disease
The joker of morality
The pioneer of slavery
The priest of sexuality
The host of violence
The Almighty fount of fear and trembling
That's the guy?
You mean to tell me on the 12th day or the 13th
that the Lord
which is to say some wiseass
got more muscle than he
reasonably
can control or figure out/some
accidental hard disk
thunderbolt/some
big mouth
woman-hating/super
heterosexist heterosexual
kind of a guy guy
he decided who could live and who would die?

And so
the names become
the names of the dead and the living
who love
Peter

John
Tede
Phil
Larry
Bob
Alan
Richard
Tom
Wayne
David
Jonathan
Bruce
Mike
Steve
And so
our names become
the names of the dead
and the living who love
Suzanne
Amy
Elizabeth
Margaret
Trude
Linda
Sara
Alexis
Frances
Nancy
Ruth
Naomi
Julie
Kate
Patricia

And out of that scriptural scattershot
our names become
the names of the dead

our names become
the names of the iniquitous
the names of the accursed
the names of the tribes of the abomination
because
my name is not Abraham
my name is not Moses/Leviticus/Solomon/Cain or Abel
my name is not Matthew/Luke/Saul or Paul
My name is not Adam
My name is female
my name is freedom
my name is the one who lives outside the tent of the father
my name is the one who is dark
my name is the one who fights for the end of the kingdom
my name is the one at home
my name is the one who bleeds
my name is the one with the womb
my name is female
my name is freedom
my name is the one the bible despised
my name is the one astrology cannot predict
my name is the name the law cannot invalidate
my name is the one who loves

and that guy
and that guy
you never even seen upclose

He cannot eat at my table
He cannot sleep in my bed

He cannot push me aside
He cannot make me commit or contemplate suicide

He cannot say my name
without shame
He cannot say my name
My name
My name is the name of the one who loves

And he
has no dominion over me
his hate has no dominion over me
I am she who will be free

And that guy
better not try to tell anybody about who
should live
and who should die
or why

His name is not holy
He is not my Lord
He is not my people
His name is not sacred
His name is not my name
His name is not the name of those who love the living

His name is not the name of those who love the living
and the dead

His name is not our name
we
who survive the death
of men and women
whose beloved

breath
becomes (at last)
our own

POEMS AGAINST A CONCLUSION

These Poems

These poems
they are things that I do
in the dark
reaching for you
whoever you are
and
are you ready?

These words
they are stones in the water
running away

These skeletal lines
they are desperate arms for my longing and love.

I am a stranger
learning to worship the strangers
around me

whoever you are
whoever I may become.

When I or Else

when I or else when you
and I or we
deliberate I lose I
cannot choose if you if
we then near or where
unless I stand as loser
of that losing possibility
that something that I have
or always want more than much
more at
least to have as less and
yes directed by desire

I guess it was my destiny to live so long

Death chase me down
death's way
uproot a breast
infest the lymph nodes
crack a femur
rip morale
to shreds

Death chase me down
death's way
tilt me off-kilter
crutch me slow
nobody show me
how
you make a cup of coffee
with no hands

Death chase me down
death's way
awkward in sunlight
single in a double bed at night
and hurtling out of mind
and out of sight

Don't chase me down
down
down
death chasing me
death's way

And I'm not done
I'm not about to blues my dues or beg

I am about to teach myself
to fly slip slide flip run
fast as I need to
on one leg

Alla Tha's All Right, but

Somebody come and carry me into a seven-day kiss
I can' use no historic no national no family bliss
I need an absolutely one to one a seven-day kiss

I can read the daily papers
I can even make a speech
But the news is stuff that tapers
down to salt poured in the breach

I been scheming about my people I been scheming about sex
I been dreaming about Africa and nightmaring Oedipus the Rex
But what I need is quite specific
terrifying rough stuff and terrific

I need an absolutely one to one a seven-day kiss
I can' use no more historic no national no bona fide family bliss
Somebody come and carry me into a seven-day kiss
Somebody come on
Somebody come on and carry me
over there!

June Jordan's "Roman Poem Number Thirteen"—near the begin-
ning of this collection—seems to me the best example of Jordan's
poetic legacy. It mixes the doom and devastation made mundane
through media exposure with the hard decision to love anyway,
because "There / is no choice in these. / Your voice / breaks very
close to me my love." In other words, the poem moves past evil to
see people, community, the possibility of romance. And this is the
trajectory we see in every poem she writes, as here:

> it is this time
> that matters
>
> it is this history
> I care about
>
> the one we make together
> awkward
> inconsistent
> as a lame cat on the loose
> or quick as kids freed by the bell

Because Jordan is a love poet in the midst of the Black Arts
Movement and the Civil Rights Movement—and in the resulting
movements these would spur on—she expresses her talent such
that what is erotically felt manifests as a singular ferocity that even
she seems surprised by: "WHAT IS THE MATTER WITH ME?
// I must become a menace to my enemies." We should be clear,
though, that Jordan's sense of resistance has its root in what we now
call intersectionality. She understands—this is important because
she publicly fought leading artists and intellectuals who did not

understand—that liberation for Black people means liberation
of the spirit, liberation for the natural world, and liberation from
imperialism. Her famous "Poem about My Rights" is at its outset a
poem about wanting to take a walk, a poem about the difficulty for
a Black woman to do what anyone does when taking a walk:

> suppose it was not here in the city but down on the beach/
> or far into the woods and I wanted to go
> there by myself thinking about God/or thinking
> about children or thinking about the world/all of it
> disclosed by the stars and the silence:

Jordan sees that it is the violation of the simplest acts that leads to
violations in housing, voting, education, and the body. And her
response embodies this vision. She writes:

> but I can tell you that from now on my resistance
> my simple and daily and nightly self-determination
> may very well cost you your life

Yes, small, mundane observations in Jordan's poems often
lead to the truth of their dire implications. And sometimes her
poetic practice moves in the opposite direction as well, leading
the reader to understand just how mundane evil has become. In
"Fourth poem from Nicaragua Libre: report from the frontier," she
writes: "when the bombs hit / leaving a patch of her hair on a piece
of her scalp / like bird's nest / in the dark yard still lit by flowers."
The use of juxtaposition, simile, and sound is extraordinary here,
but the content itself . . . for June Jordan, all the beauty of poetry
comes at a cost.

Sometimes, the beauty isn't worth the price of what some see
as normal, and Jordan's fury rises past well-wrought image to open
confrontation made through rhetorical intensity:

Tell me something
what you think would happen if
everytime they kill a black boy
then we kill a cop
everytime they kill a black man
then we kill a cop

you think the accident rate would lower
subsequently?

All this calling out, though, is so that the mundane can indeed be just that and enjoyed as such:

I might begin another list of things to do
that starts with toilet paper and
I notice that I never jot down fresh
strawberry shortcake: never
even though fresh strawberry shortcake shoots down
raisins and almonds 6 to nothing
effortlessly
effortlessly

Jordan's work carries a commitment to Black vernacular, helping pave the way for much of the contemporary work by Black writers that we read in major outlets today. She understood the phrase "standard English" to be a racist one: "There are three qualities of Black English—the presence of life, voice, and clarity—that intensify to a distinctive Black value system that we became excited about and self-consciously tried to maintain." Hence, we are fortunate to have poems that Jordan begins as only a Black person could, such as "My born on 99th Street uncle" and "Sugar come / and sugar go / Sugar dumb / but sugar know."

I believe our love for June Jordan as a poet of the people is encouraged by the ways her work reaches to protect us and by the fact that "us" knows no limits in sex, sexuality, gender, race, or location. But the root of our love is that Jordan understood herself *as* us, "I was born a Black woman / and now / I am become a Palestinian / . . . . It is time to make our way home." Her protest on behalf of the fact of bisexuality is built out of shared eros rather than antagonistic claim: "Can you give me the statistical dimensions / of your mouth on my mouth / your breasts resting on my own?" Jordan is always busy trying to be a person in love, trying to live her right to be loved:

> I wanted them to know it's not cheap
> or disgusting to love a Black
> revolutionary and
> as a matter of fact
> I wanted them to know you'd
> better love a Black revolutionary before she
> gets the idea
>
> that you don't

The legacy of June Jordan is a gift that allows us another opportunity to think not only about what poems are, but also about what poems can do. Can a poem love you?

ABOUT THE IMAGES

Images are from the June Jordan papers at the Schlesinger Library, Radcliffe Institute, unless otherwise noted.

June in 1954 on the wrought-iron railing of 681 Hancock Street in Brooklyn

The Jordan family moved from Harlem to Brooklyn when June was five. Though her father labored over the three-story brownstone, June didn't like the house very much: "Inside . . . there was tumult and hammering and scattered boxes and mops and brooms and so much confusion!" she remembered in *Soldier: A Poet's Childhood.* But just down the street, soon after they moved in, a Mr. Epps established "the first Negro-Owned business in our neighborhood. . . . It was also the first Laundromat. And my Nanny travelled from New Jersey to inspect and verify this wonder for herself. She and my mother and I made a stately beeline to that miracle we needed to behold."

June having a lot of fun at a Flamboyant Ladies Theatre Company Sunday Salon

Gwendolen Hardwick and Alexis De Veaux hosted the gatherings in their New York apartment from 1978 to 1986. June is second from left in this two-page spread, with Sara Miles at the center and Alexis De Veaux on the right.

Alexis De Veaux writes, "I do not meet June Jordan. I encounter her. The way one encounters what one cannot see—force, cosmic energy, the way, I imagine, planets, stars, other constellations encounter each other; by way of light, vibration, cruising the other's orbit" ("A Conjuring: Love Supreme: June Jordan, Love Note for JJ," *The Feminist Wire,* March 25, 2016).

We were not able to identify the three other beautiful and flamboyant ladies in this photo, or the photographer. If you know who they are, please get in touch with the editors or with Copper Canyon Press.

June and scholar/activist Angela Davis in a still from Pratibha Parmar's 1991 documentary *A Place of Rage: African American Women Who Revolutionized Society*

Angela Davis writes: "I would call her sometimes for no other reason than to feel the exhilaration of her protracted laughter. Her lifelong devotion to justice, equality and radical democracy seemed to revolve around the pleasure she felt in hurling beautiful words at a world full of racism, poverty, homophobia and inane politicians determined to preserve this awful state of affairs. There was always joy in her rage" (from "Tribute to June Jordan," *Sojourner,* July 15, 2002).

Four literary legends singing at Jackson State College in November 1973

June, Alice Walker, Lucille Clifton, and Audre Lorde at the Phillis Wheatley Poetry Festival, organized by Dr. Margaret Walker Alexander. (Lucille Clifton papers at the Manuscript, Archives, and Rare Book Library, Emory University).

June hitting the dance floor with Adrienne Rich at the Associated Writers and Writing Programs (AWP) conference in Tempe, Arizona, 1994 (AWP online photo gallery)

The world's quiver and shine
I'd clasp for you forever
jetty vanishing into pearlwhite mist
western sunstruck water light....

> —Adrienne Rich, from "For June, in the Year
> 2001," *The School Among the Ruins: Poems
> 2000–2004*

June at the Smithsonian Institute on Thursday, December 4,
1997, celebrating the Ugandan postage stamp printed in
her honor.

The other great African American writers honored with a stamp
(and in attendance) were Maya Angelou, Rita Dove, Mari Evans,
and Charles Johnson. Through E. Ethelbert Miller's coordination
with the Inter-Governmental Philatelic Corporation, Ghana and
Uganda also created stamps honoring Richard Wright, Toni Cade
Bambara, Sterling Brown, Zora Neale Hurson, Alex Haley, Henry
Louis Gates Jr., and Stephen Henderson. The proceeds went to
programs promoting literacy in Africa and the United States.

"These poems / they are things that I do in the dark...."

June stands before a poster of her signature poem. She reprinted
"These Poems" in *New Days* (1974), *Things that I Do in the Dark*
(1977), *Naming Our Destiny* (1989), and *Haruko/Love Poems* (1994),
and editors Sara Miles and Jan Heller Levi used it as the epigraph
in her collected poems, *Directed by Desire*, published posthumously
in 2005. The photograph is by Junichi P. Semitsu, June's student in
Poetry for the People at UC Berkeley. He later directed the program
for seven semesters when June was too ill to continue.

"Hi, there. My name is George / Washington/Carver. / If you will bear with me / for a few minutes I / will share with you / a few of the 30,117 uses to which / the lowly peanut has been put by me / since yesterday afternoon . . ."

Early handwritten draft of "Notes on the Peanut," dedicated to poet David Henderson and included in *Passion* (1980).

A bolder—but unused—cover design for the 1996 reissue of June's first collection of essays, *Civil Wars* (1981)

Nine portraits of June Jordan in 1981

Contact sheet by Sara Miles.

INDEX OF TITLES

INDEX OF FIRST LINES

ABOUT THE AUTHOR

June Jordan (1936–2002), born in Harlem and raised in Bedford-Stuyvesant, was a prolific and passionate activist, poet, journalist, essayist, and teacher—an essential voice on the front lines of American poetry, international political vision, and human moral witness. She was the author of more than twenty-five volumes of poetry, fiction, and essays, as well as numerous children's books. She wrote the librettos for the operas *Bang Bang Über Alles* (with music by Adrienne Torf) and *I Was Looking at the Ceiling and Then I Saw the Sky* (with music by John Adams, first directed by Peter Sellars). She also wrote lyrics for and performed with Bernice Reagon and Sweet Honey in the Rock.

Jordan's experiences teaching poetry workshops for teenagers in Brooklyn, and then joining the writing faculty of SEEK (Search for Education, Elevation, and Knowledge) at the City University of New York, inspired her radical belief in education as a tool for social change. Working with Herbert Kohl at Teachers & Writers Collaborative, with Terri Bush in Voice of the Children, and with colleagues such as Toni Cade Bambara, David Henderson, Audre Lorde, and Adrienne Rich at the City University of New York, Jordan saw teaching as part of her responsibility as a poet. After stints at Connecticut College, Sarah Lawrence College, and Yale University, she became a professor of English at the State University of New York at Stony Brook, where she directed the Poetry Center.

In 1988, she was appointed professor of African American Studies at the University of California Berkeley. There she created one of the most admired poetry programs in the country. Her Poetry for the People (P4P) demanded deep immersion in the history and practice of poetry; equally, it inspired and required community involvement. Jordan's students made poetry *for* the people and took poetry *to* the people. They gave readings but also led poetry-writing workshops through after-school programs, senior citizen centers, food programs for the homeless, and safe shelters for women. Most importantly, students listened to participants' poems, showing long-excluded populations that their voices mattered. *June Jordan's Poetry for the People: A Revolutionary Blueprint* (1995), edited by Lauren Muller and the Poetry for the People Blueprint Collective, is still in print, and P4P graduates are now all around the country and globe inspiring poetry and community collaborations.

June Jordan died from breast cancer in 2002. Through the example of her life, her teaching, her writing, her personal and political commitment, and her belief, above all, in poetry *and* people—and what people, together with poetry, can accomplish—she left a legacy of excellence and abiding hope. As she wrote, "We are the ones we have been waiting for."

ABOUT THE EDITORS

Jan Heller Levi, poet, was a student and longtime friend of June Jordan. She is, with Sara Miles, coexecutor of the June M. Jordan Literary Estate Trust. With Miles, she coedited *Directed by Desire: The Collected Poems of June Jordan,* and, with Christoph Keller, coedited *We're On: A June Jordan Reader.* She is also the editor of *A Muriel Rukeyser Reader.* She taught in the undergraduate and the MFA program in creative writing at Hunter College in New York City for many years. Her most recent book of poems, her fourth, is *That's the Way to Travel,* published in a bilingual edition (English/German) by Moloko Print in 2019. She now lives in Switzerland with her husband, Christoph Keller.

Christoph Keller—novelist, playwright, memoirist—is the executive assistant of the June M. Jordan Literary Estate Trust. With Jan Heller Levi, he edited *We're On: A June Jordan Reader,* and has worked with foreign publishers on translations of Jordan's writing into German, French, Spanish, Polish, Portuguese, and Basque. Keller also edited a Bengali and English selection of poems entitled *Only Our Hearts Will Argue Hard.* Keller's 2019 novel, *The Ground Beneath Our Feet,* won the Alemannic Literary Award; his memoir *Jeder Krüppel ein Superheld* (Every Cripple a Superhero) was published in Switzerland by Limmat Verlag in 2020.

SPECIAL THANKS

The book you are holding is a testament to the diverse community of passionate readers who supported "My Name Is My Own: Celebrating June Jordan and Ruth Stone." Copper Canyon Press is deeply grateful to the following individuals around the world whose philanthropic vision and love of poetry made this collection possible. We have published *The Essential June Jordan* together. Thank you!

Alison
Lylianna Allala
Noura Alzuabi
Melissa Anderson
Anonymous (3)
Peggy Armstrong
Elle Arra
Loretta Libby Atkins
Elizabeth Bailey
Julian Kai Barnard
Andrew Bartel
In honor of Ida Bauer, Betsy
    Gifford, and Beverly Sachar
Robert Becker
Jill Beech
Donna Bellew
In memory of Eavan Boland
Twanna P. Bolling
Partridge Boswell
Marianne Botos
In Memory of Mary Jane Brewster
Ronda Piszk Broatch
Joan Marian Broughton
Louise W. Brown
Vincent T. Buck
Claudia Cappio
Frank Carsey
Sarah and Zuzu Carson
Adrienne Cassel
Louisa Castner
Sam Chernak
MaryBeth Jarvis Clark

In memory of Catherine M. Clem
Nathan Clum
Harriett Cody and Harvey Sadis
Nan Cohen
Elizabeth J. Coleman
Graham Coppin
David Moore and J. Cortés
Phillissa Dorse
Jill Dotson
Lorraine Eakin
Elaina Ellis
Thomas Enochs
Beroz Ferrell
Laura Fjeld
Mary Warren Foulk
Garrett
Loretta Gase
Patricia Gifford
Angela B. Ginorio
Garrett Gomez, Poet
Kip Greenthal
Valyntina Grenier
Jim Halligan
Mark Hamilton and Suzie Rapp
Margaret Hooker Wagner
Susannah Hook-Rodgers
Duane Kirby Jensen
Judy Jensen
A.K.
Susan Karwoska
Mick Kligler
George Knotek

Poetry is vital to language and living. Since 1972, Copper Canyon Press has published extraordinary poetry from around the world to engage the imaginations and intellects of readers, writers, booksellers, librarians, teachers, students, and donors.

Copper Canyon Press gratefully acknowledges the kindness, patronage, and generous support of Jean Marie Lee, whose love and passionate appreciation of poetry has provided an everlasting benefit to our publishing program.

WE ARE GRATEFUL FOR THE MAJOR SUPPORT PROVIDED BY:

THE PAUL G. ALLEN
FAMILY FOUNDATION

CULTURE

Lannan

ART WORKS.

National
Endowment
for the Arts
arts.gov

OFFICE OF ARTS & CULTURE
SEATTLE

WASHINGTON STATE
ARTS COMMISSION

TO LEARN MORE ABOUT UNDERWRITING
COPPER CANYON PRESS TITLES,
PLEASE CALL 360-385-4925 EXT. 103

WE ARE GRATEFUL FOR THE MAJOR SUPPORT PROVIDED BY:

Anonymous

Jill Baker and Jeffrey Bishop

Anne and Geoffrey Barker

In honor of Ida Bauer, Betsy
Gifford, and Beverly Sachar

Donna and Matthew Bellew

Will Blythe

John Branch

Diana Broze

John R. Cahill

Sarah Cavanaugh

The Beatrice R. and Joseph A.
Coleman Foundation

The Currie Family Fund

Stephanie Ellis-Smith and Douglas
Smith

Laurie and Oskar Eustis

Austin Evans

Saramel Evans

Mimi Gardner Gates

Gull Industries Inc. on behalf of
William True

The Trust of Warren A. Gummow

William R. Hearst, III

Carolyn and Robert Hedin

Bruce Kahn

Phil Kovacevich and Eric Wechsler

Lakeside Industries Inc. on behalf
of Jeanne Marie Lee

Maureen Lee and Mark Busto

Peter Lewis and Johnna Turiano

Ellie Mathews and Carl Youngmann
as The North Press

Larry Mawby and Lois Bahle

Hank and Liesel Meijer

Jack Nicholson

Gregg Orr

Petunia Charitable Fund and
adviser Elizabeth Hebert

Gay Phinny

Suzanne Rapp and Mark Hamilton

Adam and Lynn Rauch

Emily and Dan Raymond

Jill and Bill Ruckelshaus

Cynthia Sears

Kim and Jeff Seely

Joan F. Woods

Barbara and Charles Wright

Caleb Young as C. Young Creative

The dedicated interns and
faithful volunteers of
Copper Canyon Press

Lannan Literary Selections

For two decades Lannan Foundation has supported the publication and distribution of exceptional literary works. Copper Canyon Press gratefully acknowledges their support.

LANNAN LITERARY SELECTIONS 2021

Shangyang Fang, *Burying the Mountain*

June Jordan, *The Essential June Jordan*

Laura Kasischke, *Lightning Falls in Love*

Arthur Sze, *The Glass Constellation: New and Collected Poems*

Fernando Valverde (translated by Carolyn Forché), *América*

RECENT LANNAN LITERARY SELECTIONS FROM COPPER CANYON PRESS

Mark Bibbins, *13th Balloon*

Sherwin Bitsui, *Dissolve*

Jericho Brown, *The Tradition*

Victoria Chang, *Obit*

Leila Chatti, *Deluge*

John Freeman, *Maps*

Jenny George, *The Dream of Reason*

Deborah Landau, *Soft Targets*

Rachel McKibbens, *blud*

Philip Metres, *Shrapnel Maps*

Aimee Nezhukumatathil, *Oceanic*

Camille Rankine, *Incorrect Merciful Impulses*

Paisley Rekdal, *Nightingale*

Natalie Scenters-Zapico, *Lima :: Limón*

Natalie Shapero, *Popular Longing*

Frank Stanford, *What About This: Collected Poems of Frank Stanford*

C.D. Wright, *Casting Deep Shade*

Matthew Zapruder, *Father's Day*

The Chinese character for poetry is made up of two parts:
"word" and "temple." It also serves as pressmark for
Copper Canyon Press.

The poems are set in Adobe Garamond Pro.
Book design and composition by Phil Kovacevich.